Claiming God's Promises

by Alger Fitch

You may obtain a 64-page leader's guide to accompany this paperback. Order number 41029 from Standard Publishing or your local supplier.

A Division of Standard Publishing
Cincinnati, Ohio 45231
No. 41028

Unless otherwise indicated, Scriptural quotations are from the American Standard Edition of the Revised Bible, copyright 1901 by Thomas Nelson and Sons and copyright 1929 by International Council of Religious Education.

© 1984 the STANDARD PUBLISHING Co.,
Division of STANDEX INTERNATIONAL Corp.

Library of Congress Cataloging in Publication Data

Fitch, Alger Morton.
  Claiming God's promises.

  1. God—Promises. 2. Christian life—1960-
I. Title
BT180.P7F57   1984   231   83-24379
ISBN 0-87239-750-5 (pbk.)

Printed in U.S.A.   1984

Table of Contents

Preface 4

Introduction: Standing on the Promises 5

   1 Promise of Forgiveness 13

   2 Promise of His Presence 23

   3 Promise of Newness 33

   4 Promise of Joy 42

   5 Promise of Healing 53

   6 Promise of Abundance 63

   7 Promise of Holy Spirit 72

   8 Promise of Security 83

   9 Promise of Prayer 94

   10 Promise of Guidance 105

   11 Promise of Discipline 113

   12 Promise of Christ's Return 124

   13 Promise of Victory 135

Conclusion 144

PREFACE

The gospel is "good news" because of what it promises. It contains facts about what Christ did for man. It has commands and warnings. But it becomes joyous tiding because with its facts, commands, and warnings are God's unfailing promises.

In such promises God assures you and me that what Jesus did affects us eternally and positively. Connected to His commands to all men are exhilarating promises that give each of us strength for today and bright hope for tomorrow.

At this hour of history no part of the gospel of grace can be slighted. With some lives hurting and some congregations struggling, we need to hear again God's promises that build hope and resurrect faith. Since Jesus has come into history, we are assured that He is "the mediator of a better covenant, which hath been enacted upon better promises" (Hebrews 8:6).

If dark clouds are hovering over your heart, or storms are raging in your soul, or things are not going right in your church, let the precious promises of the Bible allow the sun of hope to break into the darkness. Let each new day dawn with joy and anticipation as you claim one after another of Heaven's glorious promises.

This book is dedicated to putting a rainbow in your sky and a smile in your heart. Each chapter isolates one of the major promises the Lord has left for all of His people to enjoy. So read a chapter. Meditate on the goodness of God who gave to you such a word of hope. Praise Him for His kindness. Enjoy the inner peace that comes, and share it with some other life you are privileged to touch today.

"Having therefore these promises, beloved, let us cleanse ourselves from all defilement of flesh and spirit, perfecting holiness in the fear of God" (2 Corinthians 7:1). From Paul's day to ours we have "these promises, beloved." When they are heard in the heart, hopes build and lives change. William A. Ogden has expressed the feelings of all of us:

> Sweet are the promises, kind is the word,
> Dearer far than any message man ever heard;
>
> Trust in His promises, faithful and sure,
> Lean upon the Savior and thy soul is secure.

Introduction:
Standing on the Promises

Standing on the promises of Christ my King,
Through eternal ages let His praises ring;
Glory in the highest, I will shout and sing,
Standing on the promises of God.

Standing on the promises that cannot fail,
When the howling storms of doubt and fear assail,
By the living word of God I shall prevail,
Standing on the promises of God.
—R. Kelso Carter

   Deacon Jones has said that some folks who sing that song "Standing on the Promises" are really just sitting on the premises.[1]

   If we are to stand on God's promises, as individuals and as congregations, we need to consider again each of the divine pledges made to us by the Heavenly Father, consider it as if we were hearing the words for the first time.

   Some writers report that the Bible is filled with promises. And so it is. But it is not necessary to exaggerate, as some do. I read that the Bible has nearly thirty thousand promises. Forgive me for doubting that a book of less than thirty-two thousand verses contains thirty thousand promises. By a careful count there are 1,018 promises in

---

[1] Deacon Jones was a cartoon character in the *Lookout*, a magazine of Standard Publishing.

the New Testament. And it is obvious to any discerning reader that some of these New Covenant promises are to specific persons or groups at particular times and on certain occasions. Not all of the 1,018 are applicable to every Bible reader today.

Some of Christ's grand promises were given only to His special ambassadors, the apostles. Still there are many other promises meant for every follower of the Master to claim and enjoy.

The Scripture cries out about God's faithfulness: "When my father and my mother forsake me, then Jehovah will take me up" (Psalm 27:10). That is a promise!

The believer clings to God's word: "I will in no wise fail thee, neither will I in any wise forsake thee" (Hebrews 13:5). That is a promise!

Jesus assured His followers, "Upon this rock I will build my church; and the gates of Hades shall not prevail against it" (Matthew 16:18). That is a promise!

"I am with you always, even unto the end of the world" (Matthew 28:20). That is a promise!

"Ask, and it shall be given you; seek, and ye shall find; knock, and it shall be opened unto you" (Matthew 7:7). That is a promise!

In the following pages we shall consider some of God's special promises that certainly are made to all of us. By so doing, we will be stronger in the faith. But first let us think about why it is wise to stand on the promises of God—to build your life upon them.

Second Peter 1:3, 4 declares that Jesus our Lord "hath granted unto us all things that pertain unto life and godliness, through the knowledge of him that called us by his own glory and virtue; whereby he hath granted unto us his precious and exceeding great promises; that through these ye may become partakers of the divine nature."

Simon Peter asserts that God's promises are "precious and exceeding great." Why? It is this question that must now be answered: Why are God's promises so exceeding great?

The Promises Are Great
Because the God Who Gave Them Is Great

Upon pondering Heaven's gracious words of hope to earth, the human heart breaks out in songs like Stuart K. Hine's "How Great Thou Art." The Bible sparkles with great promises, because the God of the Scripture is so great.

The promises of the Bible are greater than promises you and I can give. Jesus made promises beyond the ability of humans to fulfill. In the Sermon on the Mount the Master Teacher guaranteed, "Seek ye first his kingdom, and his righteousness; and all these things shall be added unto you" (Matthew 6:33). Could any mere man assure another of the food, clothing, and shelter implied in the words "all these things"? I could not give such a promise. But Jesus both can and does.

In the Corinthian correspondence see these words of hope: "God is able to make all grace abound unto you; that ye, having always all sufficiency in everything, may abound unto every good work" (2 Corinthians 9:8). How similar is the encouragement to the Philippians: "And my God shall supply every need of yours according to his riches in glory in Christ Jesus" (Philippians 4:19).

We cannot make promises like that. Such assurance is beyond human ability to give. But ancient Abraham was right in "being fully assured that what he [God] had promised, he was able also to perform" (Romans 4:21).

The promises of the Almighty are greater than any human can offer. They are even greater than you and I can imagine. "As it is written, Things which eye saw not, and ear heard not, and which entered not into the heart of man, whatsoever things God prepared for them that love him," wrote the apostle (1 Corinthians 2:9).

Our eyes have seen beautiful things. Have you walked through a rose garden lately? Have you enjoyed seeing the sun set in the golden west? Have you viewed majestic hills snow-covered on the horizon?

My eyes have beheld magnificent sights in God's creation. Yet I know Paul is right. My mind without divine revelation would never have imagined what "God prepared for them that love him."

Ear has not heard. I have thrilled as choirs have sung and orchestras played. I have been awakened joyously by birds chirping in the early morning. I have heard the symphony of wind in the trees and rippling water in the stream. But my ears, like yours, have never heard anything nearly as beautiful as the gospel story with all its enrapturing promises.

My mind has not joined the scientists at NASA (National Aeronautics and Space Administration) and imagined how to get men to the moon and beyond. Nor have I been able to devise a way to get spaceships to remain in the heavens above. Much less could I ever imagine the greatness and goodness of God.

Yet while my ears have not heard, my eyes have not seen, and my mind has not imagined the graciousness of God to man, that is what the Bible promises reveal. The writings of the apostles and prophets make known a God who "is able to do exceeding abundantly above all that we ask or think" (Ephesians 3:20).

Let me say again that the promises of God are greater than I can give, greater than I can imagine, and even greater than I can contain.

Such was the promise to ancient Israel regarding tithing: "Bring ye the whole tithe into the store-house, that there may be food in my house, and prove me now herewith, saith Jehovah of hosts, if I will not open you the windows of heaven, and pour you out a blessing, that there shall not be room enough to receive it" (Malachi 3:10). Not room enough, says the Lord. Man cannot contain the abundance of God's supply.

Everyone is blessed by the Twenty-third Psalm and its comforting lines about "green pastures" and "still waters." But just now remember the words, "My cup runneth over" (verse 5). Friend, fill your heart with Christ's gospel and your life will overflow. Kindness, goodness, love, and joy will spill over from your heart to those around you. How true and righteous are God's wonderful promises! "More to be desired are they than gold, yea, than much fine gold; sweeter also than honey and the droppings of the honeycomb" (Psalm 19:10).

The Promises of God Are Sure
Because God Is Able and God Is Good

When a mortal gives a promise he may have every intention of keeping it, but just because he is mortal he may be unable to fulfill his word.

Someone asks, "Will you lend me five dollars? Payday is this Friday." And you lend the money, confident of having it back that very weekend. But on Friday night your friend says, "We were supposed to get paid today, but the boss says there will be a delay."

In a wedding ceremony people make vows that at the moment they have every intention of keeping. But in the years that follow, how many find themselves either unable or unwilling to keep their promises! This is because man is mortal. Man does not know the future. Man is often unable to do what he would like.

Worse than that, men sometimes break pledges, not because they are human, but because they are sinful. Or careless men are tricked into making promises they cannot keep. This is why we are cautioned, "Before you sign that promissory note, before you sign that contract, be sure to read the small print."

You can be sure that when the Heavenly Father speaks it is not the word of a mortal nor of a sinner. It is the word of God. As Titus 1:2 declares, God "cannot lie." It is not in His character to utter anything untrue. "It is impossible for God to lie," argues the author of the book of Hebrews (6:18). He adds, "He is faithful that promised" (10:23).

Because of God's total honesty, it has been customary in the courts to ask a witness, before he or she brings testimony, to place the right hand on the Bible, which like its divine author speaks the truth, the whole truth, and nothing but the truth. The character of God is behind all of His promises.

The promises of the Lord are great because the promiser is great. The promises from Heaven are sure, since God is not a man but is rather the able one who can carry through on everything He tells us He will do (see Mark 10:27). Never was the wise Solomon wiser than when he observed regarding God that "there hath not failed one word of all his good promise" (1 Kings 8:56). Neither was the sage Saul of Tarsus ever more confident than when he concluded, "For how many soever be the promises of God, in him [Jesus] is the yea: wherefore also through him is the Amen" (2 Corinthians 1:20).

The Promises of God Are Conditional
Because God Is Free

God has a free will. He can do as He choses. Man is God's highest creation and has been blessed by being made in God's image. Like his maker, man can think and reason, know love and joy, and make decisions. To be man (not just robot or automaton) man must be free either to accept or to refuse God's will for his life.

That is why God's promises to men are in covenant form with parties, terms, and pledges. The giving may be totally on the divine side, but the receiver must be free to reject or accept the offer on the human side. That means God's promises are conditional. Many mistakes are made by those who do not note that God's promises are, on most occasions, conditional promises.

First John 1:9 reads, "If we confess our sins, he is faithful and righteous to forgive us our sins, and to cleanse us from all unrighteousness." What is the *if* doing in the opening line of this verse? It is there to make it evident that we have here a conditional promise.

"Draw nigh to God, and he will draw nigh to you" (James 4:8) is another promise with strings attached. "Ask, and it shall be given you" (Matthew 7:7) is still another promise with terms to be met on the human side.

The late James Earl Ladd, who was a noted evangelist in the Pacific Northwest, preached a sermon entitled "All God's Promises Got Strings." The thought was borrowed from the old spiritual, "All God's Chillun Got Shoes." Maybe not "all" of God's promises are conditional, but many of them are, if not most of them.

There are divinely given conditions for national salvation, personal salvation, and eternal salvation.

Some modern interpreters see a fulfillment of prophetic promise in the Jews' return to Palestine in modern times, even a return in unbelief and not in repentance. Should such be the case, the beneficiaries of the promise will do well to give heed to an ancient promise to Israel that began with the word *if*. *If* is a very small word that has a very big meaning. "If my people, who are called by my name, shall humble themselves, and pray, and seek my face, and turn from their wicked ways; then will I hear from heaven, and will forgive their sin, and will heal their land" (2 Chronicles 7:14). *If* is a word God joined to national salvation.

Are there *ifs* wedded also to the promises of personal salvation? Jesus is the promiser of Mark 16:15, 16. "Go ye into all the world, and preach the gospel to the whole creation. He that believeth and is baptized shall be saved; but he that disbelieveth shall be condemned." The Great Commission promise is a conditional promise.

Peter, who understood this, stood up to speak on the first day of the church, as recorded in Acts 2. He announced the good news "that whosoever shall call on the name of the Lord shall be saved" (verse 21). Salvation is for those who call on the Lord's name.

When people called out to Christ's apostles, "What shall we do?" (verse 37), Peter and the other ambassadors of the King clarified how you "call on the name of the Lord." They spoke their words "as the Spirit gave them utterance" (verse 4). Here are those words: "Repent ye, and be baptized every one of you in the name of Jesus Christ unto the remission of your sins; and ye shall receive the gift of the Holy Spirit. For to you is the promise, and to your children, and to all that are afar off, even as many as the Lord our God shall call unto him" (verses 38, 39). By divine authority Peter laid down conditions to be met.

A young recruit was learning parachute jumping. He was told authoritatively, "You will jump when I say 'jump.' Count to ten and pull the cord on your right shoulder. If the chute should fail to open, there is no need to get excited. Simply count to ten again and this time pull the cord on your left shoulder. I'll be down below ready to pick you up in the red truck."

The recruit made his very first jump. He counted to ten and pulled the cord on his right shoulder as instructed. Nothing happened as he descended swiftly through the air. Like a professional, he counted to ten the second time and yanked at the left-shoulder cord. Still not a thing happened. At that point the rookie suspicioned, "I'll bet that fellow won't even be there to meet me in the red truck."

If one or two of God's promises had failed, we might have our doubts about others. But not even one has ever failed. When God makes a promise, He is going to keep it. But when He makes a clear and sure promise, listen for the conditions.

At many funerals the deceased is "preached into Heaven" with little regard for the conditions attached to the Scriptural promise of Heaven. God, indeed, has offered salvation freely to everybody, but one must respond with faith and obedience as the Savior asked in His gracious offer. His salvation promise has conditions to be met.

Regarding eternal salvation we read, "Be thou faithful unto death, and I will give thee the crown of life" (Revelation 2:10). After the big fisherman, Peter, admonishes his readers to add to their faith, he warns, "Brethren, give the more diligence to make your calling and election sure: for if ye do these things, ye shall never stumble: for thus shall be richly supplied unto you the entrance into the eternal kingdom of our Lord and Savior Jesus Christ" (2 Peter 1:10, 11).

God makes promises; but when we accept Jesus as our Lord and Savior, we make promises too. People respond to the invitation and come to receive the Master as Lord of their lives. Yet future days find some of them not assembling with any regularity with other believers for work or worship. Did they promise to make Jesus Lord of all, and then fail to let Him be Lord at all?

God covenants to save forever those who enter into Christ and abide in Christ. Jesus did not leave us a list of optional commandments from which we are free to select a percentage that we are willing to obey. He said, "If ye love me, ye will keep my commandments" (John 14:15). He does not always give reasons with each order. He rather gives promises. He who steps out on the all-sufficient promises enters a joy unspeakable and full of glory.

The Promises of God Are Available
Because God Is Love

God is great, so His promises are great. God is good, so His promises are sure. He is as good as His word. God is free, so, making man in His image, He has given to man a free will. He will not force upon any man a contract or covenant that this man does not choose to accept. God is also love, so every person hearing the gospel finds the offered salvation available. It is waiting just to be received.

Our maker offers salvation to one and all, but we must be willing to respond to the offer of redemption, forgiveness, and eternal life. The very word *gift* suggests both a giver and a receiver. And God is ready—yes, more than ready—to do the giving. But you and I have to be ready to accept the freely-offered gift with a heart willing to receive and obey.

This is the question to which we always must come. Are we ready for what God offers us at this very moment? God's promises are available because of His never-failing love. Do I, in appreciation, love Him to the degree that I am ready to say yes to His astounding offers to me? Can I respond sincerely with John E. Bode's poetic promise?

> O Jesus, Thou hast promised
>   To all who follow Thee
> That where Thou art in glory
>   There shall Thy servant be:
> And, Jesus, I have promised
>   To serve Thee to the end;
> O give me grace to follow
>   My Master and my Friend.

1

Five Elements of Forgiveness

for**GIVE**ness

for**GIVEN**ess

f**OR**giveness

FORgiveness

forg**I**veness

1

The Promise of Forgiveness

> If I have wounded any soul today,
> Dear Lord, Forgive!

We sing about forgiveness, we pray about forgiveness as Jesus taught us to do. We pray, "Our Father who art in heaven," as we intercede regarding His name, His kingdom, and His will. Then after requesting our daily bread, we plead, "Forgive us our debts, as we also have forgiven our debtors" (Matthew 6:9-12).

We find the theme of forgiveness makes for great music and great prayer, because it is one of God's great promises. Review in your mind some of the uplifting Bible texts on God's forgiveness, the divine pardon, and the remission of man's sins.

Isaiah, the evangelist of the prophets, pleaded with the people, "Seek ye Jehovah while he may be found; call ye upon him while he is near: let the wicked forsake his way, and the unrighteous man his thoughts; and let him return unto Jehovah, and he will have mercy upon him; and to our God, for he will abundantly pardon" (Isaiah 55:6, 7).

Luke closes his Gospel with some of the last words of Jesus prior to His ascension into Heaven. Christ asked "that repentance and remission of sins should be preached in his name unto all the nations, beginning from Jerusalem" (Luke 24:47). Luke's second volume, the book of Acts, records the preaching of that forgiveness from Jerusalem to Rome. When the Jews in Jerusalem heard the glad announcement of forgiveness through Christ, they were told, "Repent ye, and be baptized every one of you in the name of Jesus Christ unto the remission of your sins" (Acts 2:38). In the same manner, when Gentiles were brought to the Savior, the apostle promised that "through his [Christ's] name every one that believeth on him shall receive remission of sins" (Acts 10:43). Even in distant Colossae the converts gloried that, in Christ, they had "redemption, the forgiveness of . . . sins" (Colossians 1:14).

The aged apostle John loved his people and penned for them this assurance: "I write unto you, my little children, because your sins are forgiven you" (1 John 2:12). Earlier in the same letter, he had reminded the Christians of their need for constant cleansing and pardon. He included his own need when he said, "If we confess our sins, he is faithful and righteous to forgive us our sins, and to cleanse us from all unrighteousness" (1 John 1:9).

Forgiveness is a promise. Forgiveness is a promise from God. Forgiveness is a promise to you and to me. We can learn more of its meaning by observing other words found within the word itself.

The *Give* in Forgiveness

Have you ever noticed that in the very center of the term *forgiveness* is the significant word *give*?

To comprehend divine forgiveness, one must call to mind all that it was necessary for God to give to make the forgiveness possible. John 3:16, "the gospel in a nutshell," reads, "For God so loved the world, that he gave." What the Heavenly Father gave was "his only begotten Son."

The very Creator, who gave us the galaxies and our earth upon which we dwell, also gave His unique Son to live among us. He gave that Son in death for us. He also gave His Spirit to indwell us. He gave the message of the gospel to us that we might know the way of salvation. There would be no consideration today of this word *forgiveness* were it not for God's giving His Son in the middle of history.

For the endurance of Christian homes, the apostle Paul admonished, "Husbands, love your wives, even as Christ also loved the church, and *gave* himself up for it" (Ephesians 5:25). Frances E. Havergal has put Jesus' gift into rhyme:

> I gave My life for thee,
>   My precious blood I shed,
> That thou might'st ransomed be,
>   And quickened from the dead;
> I gave, I gave My life for thee—
>   What hast thou giv'n for Me?

An excuse-maker is reported to have said that he refused to go to church any more because all he ever heard there was "give, give, give." The response from the preacher was, "Sir, I want to thank you for the best definition of Christianity I have ever heard."

God is ever giving. And what can the appreciative person do in response but give time, money, talent, and life that others may learn of God's loving forgiveness? In the heart of that forgiveness is the giving of God. "Thanks be to God for his unspeakable gift" (2 Corinthians 9:15). Is it any wonder that, through the centuries, the cross has become the symbol of Christianity? Could it have been otherwise, when Jesus taught, "The Son of man also came . . . to give his life a ransom for many"? (Mark 10:45).

The *Given* in Forgiveness

There are in the word *forgiveness* four letters G-I-V-E. Look with me now at the five letters G-I-V-E-N.

In a public debate the speakers do not argue about every phase of a subject. There are certain facts upon which all agree. The non-debatable, the "given," are the universally-agreed-upon points. These are statements accepted by both parties.

On the subject of divine forgiveness, what is "given," or conceded, by all? The fact beyond debate is that forgiveness is in the mind of God, not in the body of man. Let me repeat that thought. When forgiveness takes place, it does not take place in the person that needs forgiveness. It rather happens in the person doing the forgiving. It occurs in the one who has been sinned against. This being true, God's forgiveness of man takes place in Heaven, not on earth.

To say, "I know I am forgiven, because I feel it within," is to mislocate the wonderful fact. Forgiveness is not in my nervous system or in your heart; it is in God's mind.

Try to imagine the unimaginable. Attempt to visualize my wife and me in a heated argument. I might later wonder if she had forgiven me for some harsh words spoken. Do you see the dilemma? I could go around for days feeling unforgiven, when in reality I was forgiven long ago. It is equally possible that I might feel completely forgiven, when in reality she had not forgiven me. Since forgiveness takes place in the one sinned against, how will I know if I am forgiven? I may feel unforgiven when I am forgiven. I may feel forgiven when I am not forgiven. So I will know I am forgiven only when my wife tells me in so many words that I am.

You know you have sinned against God. If you want to know if He has forgiven you, you ought not to look at how you inwardly feel about it. Rather you should listen to the Word of God. You should hearken to the conditions upon which the Lord promises His forgiveness. Pay heed to Christ's clear statements as to when forgiveness is granted.

A preacher in Oklahoma many years ago was telling his audience that he knew he was saved because he could feel it within. Drinking from a glass of water on the pulpit, he illustrated: "How do I know this water is good? It tastes good and it feels good all the way down."

What destroyed his argument, and almost destroyed him, was that he later became deathly ill with typhoid fever. Authorities tested the well from which the water in the pulpit glass had been drawn, and there the cause of infection was found. The water that had tasted good and felt good was not good by scientific standards. Likewise our feelings must be corrected by the guiding Word of God.

Romans 8:16 reads, "The Spirit himself beareth witness with our spirit, that we are children of God." Note that the preposition in this sentence is *with* and not *unto*. Paul is not speaking of one witness, but of two. He is not making the human spirit the listener, but one of the two who testify. The apostle is not suggesting that subjectively, down inside my being, I feel the Spirit moving. He rather is referring to words of testimony from the divine Spirit first and then from the spirit of man. These are the two spirits on the witness stand—the divine Spirit and the human spirit. The Holy Spirit lays down in His testimony the terms of forgiveness. The individual testifies, "I have met Christ's conditions, and so I know I am forgiven."

The *Or* in Forgiveness

The *give* in our forgiveness is the giving of Christ who went to Calvary. The *given* in our forgiveness is the fact that forgiveness takes place in the mind of God above. Now it is time to call attention to a two-letter word in the term *forgiveness*. That is the little word *or*.

Will it be this or that? Will it be life or death? Will it be, for you, a matter of repent or perish? (see Luke 13:3). God offers alternatives. If you choose forgiveness, there is everlasting life. If you decide not to accept God's forgiveness, there is everlasting death. Hear again the very words of Jesus as He orders the message to be preached to all the world: "He that believeth and is baptized shall be saved; but he that disbelieveth shall be condemned" (Mark 16:16). We have the alternatives. We can select the road we travel. The road we choose determines our destination.

The good news is this: "There is therefore now no condemnation to them that are in Christ Jesus" (Romans 8:1). Here is an obvious choice. We can be "in Christ Jesus" or out of Christ. When Jesus comes back from Heaven, He will be "rendering vengeance to them that know not God, and to them that obey not the gospel" (2 Thessalonians 1:8). Obeying and disobeying are the alternatives with eternal consequences. "The wages of sin is death; but the free gift of God is eternal life in Christ Jesus our Lord" (Romans 6:23). Death and life are my options, and they are yours.

Early in your life you may have memorized John 3:16 about the love of God. When we look again, not just to that single verse but to the entire third chapter, we find that Nicodemus was startled to learn that even a man in his high religious position "must be born anew" (John 3:1-7). But note with precision the bottom line with which the chapter ends. There are held out two clear alternatives; "He that believeth on the Son hath eternal life; but he that obeyeth not the Son shall not see life, but the wrath of God abideth on him" (John 3:36).

I could not be a faithful teacher of the Word if I failed to give both halves of the whole story. The full gospel contains wonderful promises, and it gives dreadful warnings. The world must be made aware that God's arms are outstretched to all, no matter who they are or what they have done. He is ready, willing, and able to forgive. But we owe it to all men to let them know that it is possible to sin against one's very self by spurning the offer. There will remain but the alternative of "the wrath of God."

John the Baptist put it this way: "I indeed baptize you in water unto repentance: but he that cometh after me is mightier than I . . . he shall baptize you in the Holy Spirit and in fire" (Matthew 3:11). John seems to be telling the multitudes at the Jordan River that there is before them an option regarding the Messiah. Either they will be responsive to Him and be gathered like valuable wheat into the garner of Heaven, or they will reject Him and be burned like chaff or an unfruitful tree (see verses 10 and 12 and compare Revelation 21:8 and Matthew 25:41 and 46). Those are the choices regarding God's forgiveness. It is either eternal separation from God or eternal life with God. We must choose. "Choose life" (Deuteronomy 30:19).

King Agrippa, when confronted with the choice, said to Paul, "With but little persuasion thou wouldest fain make me a Christian" (Acts 26:28). The *King James Version* translates Agrippa's response as "almost thou persuadest me to be a Christian." This wording led P. P. Bliss to write the invitation hymn that begins:

> "Almost persuaded" now to believe;
> "Almost persuaded" Christ to receive.

But the song concludes:

> "Almost" cannot avail;
> "Almost" is but to fail!
> Sad, sad, that bitter wail,
> "Almost," but lost!

The *For* in Forgiveness

To better understand the concept of forgiveness, give your attention to another word within that word. Look at the *for* in *forgiveness*. What does a human being need to do for the forgiveness of sins? What was it necessary for Jesus to do for the forgiveness of man's sins?

With such a question before us, the mind is attracted as if by magnetic pull to Hebrews 9:22: "Apart from shedding of blood there is no remission." This explains why it was necessary for Christ to die "for our sins according to the scriptures" (1 Corinthians 15:3). This is why Jesus, at the institution of the Lord's Supper, "took a cup, and gave thanks, and gave to them, saying, Drink ye all of it; for this is my blood of the covenant, which is poured out for many unto remission of sins" (Matthew 26:27, 28). Here is the answer to our question of what Christ did for our forgiveness. He shed His blood. He gave His life (see Leviticus 17:11).

Knowing what God has given for our forgiveness, we need yet to discover what the New Testament tells us we must do to receive God's freely offered pardon.

It is essential that we divide the question. The answer of the Spirit is different when the sinner needing forgiveness is a Christian and when the sinner is one who has not previously given his life to Christ. We make this distinction because the Scriptures make this distinction.

The epistles in the New Testament are addressed to people in the body of Christ, not to people out of Christ. It is a mistake to read 1 John 1:9, which was written to believers, and then to apply that promise to unbelievers. Good hermeneutical principles require that we ask, "Who is speaking?" and "To whom is he speaking?"

The apostle John is writing to Christians like himself when he says, "If we say that we have no sin, we deceive ourselves, and the truth is not in us. If we confess our sins, he is faithful and righteous to forgive us our sins, and to cleanse us from all unrighteousness" (1 John 1:8, 9).

A Christian falling into a trespass needs but to confess the wrong to his Savior. To this counsel of John to the believer agrees the admonition of Peter to the disciple Simon: "Repent therefore of this thy wickedness, and pray the Lord, if perhaps the thought of thy heart shall be forgiven thee" (Acts 8:22).

The Christian, at any sin, is to repent and ask forgiveness. Is that what aliens from God's kingdom are asked to do? Since the book of Acts is the account of how the apostolic church sought to carry out the Lord's Great Commission, we note with interest that no non-Christian was ever admonished simply to confess his sin in a sinner's prayer. In the ten cases of conversion that Luke records in Acts, hearers of the gospel were brought to faith, to repentance, and to the waters of baptism. All of these responses were recorded of the converts from Jerusalem to the uttermost parts of the earth. All these words were used by Christ in His orders (see Matthew 28:19; Mark 16:16; Luke 24:47).

The first case of conversion in Christian history is given in detail so that it may stand as a pattern for all. When three thousand hearers came to believe that Jesus was "Lord and Christ" (Acts 2:36), they inquired what they were to do (verse 37). No apostle replied that there were no terms to be met. Rather Peter, answering for all the twelve, said, "Repent ye, and be baptized every one of you in the name of Jesus Christ." Immediately, before Peter reached the period in his sentence, he added the reason for these requested actions: "unto the remission of your sins" (verse 38).

Give full attention to these six words "unto the remission of your sins." Some earnest Bible students have such an exalted idea of God's sovereignty that they conclude there is nothing—absolutely nothing—that a man can do to be saved. They would reword Acts 2:38 so that it would not say that repentance and baptism are *for* or *unto* the forgiveness of sins but rather *because of* the fact that the person is already forgiven.

I am helped out of this confusion by comparing Scripture with Scripture. In Matthew 26:28, both in the original Greek and in the English translation, there is a parallel of Acts 2:38. In the former, Jesus explains why He will shed His blood. It will be *unto* or *for* remission of sins. In Acts 2:38 the same reason is given for the new believer's repentance and baptism. They also are said to be *unto* or *for* remission of sins.

Can Matthew 26:28 mean that Jesus died *because* the world was forgiven already? Or does it mean that He shed His blood *in order to obtain* the forgiveness? It obviously must mean the second. On the divine side, Jesus had to come and die so our sins can be forgiven. On the human side, the recipient has to respond in the obedience of faith that God has asked.

The *I* in Forgiveness

Fix your eyes on the word *forgiveness* until you find one more word important to our understanding. Meet the word of a single letter. Meet in the heart of *forgiveness* the personal pronoun *I*. Apply it to yourself.

Can you say, "I have been forgiven"? It is insufficient to know in general about God's forgiveness. It is not enough that others have been pardoned. You need to be able to have this assurance: "Yes, *I* am forgiven."

Are you capable of saying with Paul, "I have been crucified with Christ; and it is no longer I that live, but Christ liveth in me"? (Galatians 2:20). Are you able to put the personal pronoun where David put it in the Twenty-third Psalm: "Jehovah is *my* shepherd; *I* shall not want . . . *I* shall dwell in the house of Jehovah for ever"? (verses 1, 6).

Christ died, indeed, for every person in the world. He offers forgiveness to all. But have you personally received that forgiveness?

"Blessed is he whose transgression is forgiven, whose sin is covered" (Psalm 32:1).

Every one who has claimed God's promise of forgiveness can join in singing the great song that ends, "Praise God, my sins are gone."

Friends brought a paralytic to Jesus. Jesus said to Him, "Son, be of good cheer; thy sins are forgiven." Certain scribes called that blasphemy, since only God can forgive sins. Jesus responded, "Which is easier, to say, Thy sins are forgiven; or to say, Arise, and walk? But that ye may know that the Son of man hath authority on earth to forgive sins (then saith he to the sick of the palsy), Arise, and take up thy bed, and go unto thy house" (Matthew 9:1-8).

In this Gospel account we meet a man who could say, "I have been forgiven!" We may find also a throng of Pharisees, Sadducees, Essenes, and Herodians who had heard of forgiveness. Yet they could not say the glad words, "I have been forgiven!"

Lo, I am with you

on mountaintops
across separating borders
in Christian gatherings
through stormy darkness
in flaming judgment
down lonely roads
by new-filled tombs
beneath heavy burdens

2

The Promise of His Presence

I cannot vouch for that saying, "An apple a day keeps the doctor away." Yet I can claim that if you feast on the assurance of but one promise a week you will live on a mountain peak. Ponder for several days on God's majestic pledge of cleansing, or life, or healing, and you cannot help being elevated to the heights. The promise of God's presence, which we give attention to now, ought to lift us to "the third heaven" (see 2 Corinthians 12:2).[1]

The prophet Isaiah not only foretold the Messiah's virgin birth in Isaiah 7:14, but also predicted the name *Immanuel*. That name means *God with us* (Matthew 1:23).

It should be no surprise to us that He whose name means "God with us" should close His incarnate ministry with the promise, "Lo, I am with you always, even unto the end of the world" (Matthew 28:20). If you walk in His way, there is no circumstance in which He will not be with you. There is no place where He will not be with you. There is no time when He will not be with you.

It matters not whether you are in a work room or a worship room. He will be with you. It matters not whether you are in a court room, a hospital room, or a hotel room. He will be with you. If you are His disciple, you have the promise: "I am with you."

---

[1] There is the heaven where birds fly, the heaven where stars are placed, and the heaven spoken of as the throne room of God.

A church paper told the imaginary story of a person talking to Christ. The man said, "Jesus, as we have walked together, I have seen behind us two sets of footprints, mine and Yours. Yet I have noted also that occasionally there has been but one set of footprints. Jesus, why did You break Your promise? Why did You not stay with me always?"

Gently the Lord responded, "In those places where you saw but one set of footprints, they were mine. While you were undergoing some very difficult times, I was carrying you."

> Walking in sunlight, all of my journey;
>   Over the mountains, thro' the deep vale;
> Jesus has said, "I'll never forsake thee,"
>   Promise divine that never can fail.
> —H. J. Zelley

Christ Will Be With You on Mountaintops

In Jesus' ministry He gathered around Him disciples who had the job of walking with Him day by day. Often He took them up to some mountaintop. They were with Him as He and a caravan from Galilee ascended from Jericho up to Jerusalem for the Passover celebration. In the ascent to Mount Zion and the temple they would sing with other celebrants the ancient psalms, especially the songs of ascents (Psalms 120 through 134). At such feasts Jesus and His chosen apostles shared mountaintop experiences at the temple mount.

Sometimes while staying in the vicinity of Jerusalem, the Teacher would take His disciples out of the city and across the brook Kidron to the east. There they would ascend the Mount of Olives to the Garden of Gethsemane. "Beneath the old olive trees" Christ's followers shared mountaintop experiences of prayer.

One day Jesus took His chosen men to a special mountain in Galilee. There He delivered in their hearing the famous Sermon on the Mount, recorded in Matthew, chapters 5—7. I am convinced that each apostle knew in his heart that he was sharing in a mountaintop experience of learning at the feet of the Master Teacher. Jesus opened their minds to the Scripture, and they saw God's design as never before.

Coming down from the mountaintop experience of the transfiguration, the inner circle of Peter, James, and John found their fellow apostles in a valley of failure. The three had been on a high mountain, perhaps Mount Hermon, and had seen Jesus in His majestic deity. "He was transfigured before them; and his face did shine as the sun, and his garments became white as the light" (Matthew 17:2). "His garments became glistering, exceeding white, so as no fuller on earth can whiten them" (Mark 9:3).

Their eyes had beheld Christ's glory. Their ears had heard the voice of the Father acclaim Jesus as His Son. Their hearts desired to stay on the mountaintop. But Jesus insisted that they go down into the valley. There they met the other apostles, who had been failing in their ministry of casting out demons. Please observe that this failure was not the end of the story. Now Christ's presence was with them again. Now in the very valley of previous failure they had the mountaintop experience of seeing a demon-possessed boy set free by their Savior. When Christ is there, on mountain or in valley, failure can turn to success.

Christ Will Be With You Across Separating Borders

The promise, "Lo, I am with you always," was preceded by the assignment, "Make disciples of all the nations" (Matthew 28:19). After the order to evangelize, baptize, and catechize (or teach) across national borders, came the promise of His presence to those who carry out His instruction to take His gospel across every ethnic border. His people are to bear the good news to the uttermost part of the earth and to the whole creation (Acts 1:8; Mark 16:15), and He will be with them all the way.

Have you noticed in the reading of John 4:3, 4 that, in going from Judea into Galilee, Jesus "must needs pass through Samaria"? What kind of a "must" is that? Most Jews in their travels bypassed Samaria at all cost. They would go out of their way to cross the Jordan River and escape any dealings with Samaritans. Not Jesus! He "must needs pass through Samaria." He loves all people. This is a moral "must." It is an evangelistic urge, a soul-winning inner drive. Jesus has to go touch lives that others will neglect.

In Samaria He finds a woman at a well. He has already crossed the racial border, now He crosses the sexual border and as a male He converses with a female. Then He daringly crosses the ultimate border. He whose life is complete righteousness speaks to her whose life is total unrighteousness. That same Savior today goes with you and me when we cross borders to carry out His mission to reach the lost.

With assurance we can sing along with C. Austin Miles,

> If Jesus goes with me I'll go
> Anywhere!

Or we can pray with Washington Gladden,

> O Master, let me walk with Thee
> In lowly paths of service free.

Especially we can use these lines as we plead to be used in rescuing others:

> Help me the slow of heart to move
> By some clear, winning word of love;
> Teach me the wayward feet to stay,
> And guide them in the homeward way.

Are the congregations on America's west coast reaching the Asians who in a few years may make up the majority of that population? If your church is located in the Southwest, does it reflect the population shift by including Mexican Americans? Wherever you live—North, South, East, or West, if Christ lives in your midst, you will cross the borders to all whom God sends your way.

The church that was told to "go . . . into all the world" (Mark 16:15) needs to see that, at this time, the whole world seems to be coming to it. It is time to awaken to that promise of Jesus to be with us as we cross all borders. We, with His presence, can win both those to whom we go and those who come to us.

Christ Will Be With You in Christian Gatherings

"Assembling together" is a Christian practice to be ever encouraged and never neglected (see Hebrews 10:25). One supreme reason is the promise of Jesus: "Where two or three are gathered together in my name, there am I in the midst of them" (Matthew 18:20). Each Lord's Day, when the Lord's people gather together in the Lord's house to observe the Lord's Supper, they have the promise of His presence. Be the number gathered two or three hundred, two or three thousand, or simply two or three, He is there as He said He would be.

This pledge of His presence saw fulfillment as early as the day of Christ's resurrection. That evening, "the first day of the week . . . when the doors were shut where the disciples were, for fear of the Jews, Jesus came and stood in the midst" (John 20:19). One week later the disciples, including Thomas, were again gathered behind closed doors, and again "Jesus . . . stood in the midst" (verse 26).

When we gather together in a large or small crowd, with or without some Thomas present, Jesus is there as He committed himself to be. The gathering together to break bread on the first day of the week (Acts 20:7) is not a memorial service for a dead Christ, but a communion service with the living Christ. At the establishing of the Old Covenant, Jehovah pledged, "In every place where I record my name [or, cause my name to be remembered] I will come unto thee and I will bless thee" (Exodus 20:24). As we remember in His name the New Covenant in His blood (Matthew 26:27, 28), it is certainly to be expected that His presence and blessing will be with us as well.

Christ Will Be With You Through Stormy Darkness

Rest assured that He who is with us on mountaintops, across borders, and in Christian assemblies will be with us through the storms of life.

Such a storm is recorded in Matthew 14:24-33. Right in the middle of the Sea of Galilee, the disciples find themselves in the darkness of the night. Among them are experts at sailing, such as the fishermen Jesus has called to fish for men. Yet the distressing waves of storm and the contrary winds fill them with startling fear. It is no trifling squall. It is more to be called a tempest. But the Bible account ends with their fears gone and the waves at rest, because Jesus comes to them walking on the sea, dispelling fear and calming winds.

These same verses tell of Peter's attempt to walk on the water. Have you tried that lately? Nothing supportive is under your feet. You are going down. The waters threaten to close over your head. Perhaps you have not literally stepped out on a stormy sea, but in your personal experience there have been threatening times, impossible situations.

What is to be done when your back is against the wall? What can be tried when the bottom drops out of everything? What hope is there when you are sinking under the troubled waters for the third time? What rescue can be expected when it appears you are totally alone, and no person is near that can come to your aid? In times like these you need to cling to the promise, "I am with you always." That includes dark and stormy times.

> Will your anchor hold in the storms of life,
> When the clouds unfold their wings of strife?
> When the strong tides lift, and the cables strain,
> Will your anchor drift, or firm remain?
> —Priscilla J. Owens

It is essential for you to understand that each life will have its times of storm. We must not kid ourselves. Becoming a Christian does not guarantee that from henceforth no trials will come your way. It rather assures you that when troubles come Jesus will be there and you will not be alone.

Are we not promised in Psalm 23 "green pastures" and "still waters" when the Lord is our shepherd? An unknown poet has made a sage observation in his probing questions and clear insights:

> "In pastures green"? Not always. Sometimes He
> Who knoweth best in kindness leadeth me
> In weary ways where heavy shadows be.
>
> "By waters still"? It is not always so.
> Ofttimes the heavy tempests round me blow,
> And o'er my soul the waves and billows go.
>
> But when the storms beat loudest, and I cry
> Aloud for help, my Master standeth by
> And whispers to my soul, "Lo, it is I."
>
> So where He leadeth I can safely go,
> And in the blest hereafter I shall know
> Why in His wisdom He hath led me so.

What a grand affirmation is that statement by Jesus: "Let not your heart be troubled: believe in God, believe also in me" (John 14:1). But one must confess those words are easier to say and obey when the sun is shining, the birds are singing, and all is right in your world. Yet Jesus spoke them into the ears of His men just before the dark hours of His crucifixion. Disciples of Jesus need to "believe in God" and not allow their hearts to "be troubled." They must learn to trust that He will be with them as promised, whether in heavenly sunlight or in stormy darkness. Every raging tempest is in His power; and with assurance we can say to Him as the psalmist said to Jehovah, "Even the darkness hideth not from thee, but the night shineth as the day: the darkness and the light are both alike in thee" (Psalm 139:12).

Christ Will Be With You in Flaming Judgment

We can be confident that He who is with us through dark times here will at the end time be by our side when we pass through the fire of the Judgment Day.

The ancient book of Daniel tells of three men, Shadrach, Meshach, and Abed-nego. Many a modern quartet sings of these heroes "who wouldn't budge, they wouldn't bow, they wouldn't burn." Nebuchadnezzar's fiery furnace could not destroy them. The king in astonishment cried to his counsellors, "Did not we cast three men bound into the midst of the fire? . . . Lo, I see four men loose, walking in the midst of the fire, and they have no hurt; and the aspect of the fourth is like a son of the gods" (Daniel 3:24, 25).

When a flaming tongue of criticism makes charges against you in this world or Satan hurls fiery accusations at you in the judgment to come, the Son of God will be with you in the flames. Christ's disciples felt the fire of condemnation when Pharisees accused them of violating the Sabbath in eating from the grain fields (Matthew 12:1, 2). Jesus immediately went to their defense (verses 3-8).

In the coming great judgment, the same Savior will be for us "an Advocate with the Father" (1 John 2:1). When the devil points to each flaw in your life and mine, Jesus will protect us from every charge. The word *parakletos,* or paraclete, is often translated *comforter* or *helper.* It literally refers to *one called to your side.* In sorrow your need is for a comforter to come to your side. But in sickness the need is for a doctor, in loneliness for a friend, in legal trouble for an attorney. Jesus' presence meets whatever need you have.

The apostle John in his first epistle lifts the hearts of his readers by suggesting that on Judgment Day their judge will be their concerned "Father"; their attorney will be "Jesus Christ"; and the case will be not their wickedness but the righteousness of Him who is the "propitiation" for their sins (1 John 2:1, 2).

Christ Will Be With You Down Lonely Roads

It may be that long years have passed since the last time someone singed your soul with fiery criticism. In your case it may be rather that you suffer from not being noticed at all. Often, by outliving associates and family, the elderly live in a private room surrounded by four walls that neither talk nor listen. Loneliness is the curse of many old people. It can be also the bane of child or teenager. To go down that lonesome road all alone, at any age, pains the soul. But a child of God is not alone.

Acts, chapter 8, tells of an Ethiopian riding his chariot down the road from Jerusalem to Gaza. Luke describes the road with the words, "the same is desert" (Acts 8:26). The word *desert* is not meant to conjure up visions of the Sahara or Gobi Desert. The same word is used of a place near the Sea of Galilee where there was "much grass" (Mark 6:35, 39; John 6:10). It means a deserted place, a lonely, unpopulated area. But read the details of what would be invisible to the human eye. An angel of the Lord sent the evangelist Philip to that lonely road (Acts 8:26). The Spirit of God was there to bring Philip and the Ethiopian together (verse 29). The traveler was not in fact alone as he went down that lonely road.

John 20:11-18 lies behind the hymn in which we picture ourselves in the garden alone, but not alone, for Jesus walks and talks with us. There are times in early morning hours when you may feel alone. But the Lord keeps His promise, and you are not alone.

Christ Will Be With You by New-Filled Tombs

"Lo, I am with you always"; every hour, every day, every moment. Perhaps recently, in some cemetery, you have stood by that newly-prepared burial place. Tears filled eyes of the bereaved and their friends. Did the tears blur the fact that Christ was there as promised?

The eleventh chapter of John describes the scene as Jesus comes to the place where His friend Lazarus has been buried. Friends are there, relatives are there, and tears are there (John 11:1-44). Misunderstandings and criticisms are there also. Both Martha (verse 21) and Mary (verse 32) could not keep the words back: "Lord, if thou hadst been here, my brother had not died."

In the shortest verse in all the Bible is one of the biggest truths: "Jesus wept" (verse 35). The tears of the Master were not because death is final and life beyond is empty. You may see other reasons, but I believe the tears in Christ's eyes were because such dear friends could believe, even momentarily, that He didn't care.

When you lay to rest the one who on earth has been your life-long friend and companion, sing both the question and answer of this beautiful hymn by Frank E. Graeff:

> Does Jesus care when I've said good-bye
>   To the dearest on earth to me,
> And my sad heart aches till it nearly breaks—
>   Is it aught to Him? does He see?
>
> O yes, He cares; I know He cares!
>   His heart is touched with my grief;
> When the days are weary, the long nights dreary,
>   I know my Savior cares.

Christ Will Be With You Beneath Heavy Burdens

What about times when you feel so weak and the burdens are so heavy? Since hymns have been called the holiest thoughts of the holiest men at their holiest moments, we often turn to their wording of Bible teaching. They often speak to the heart in that they express the faith that does reside even in our broken hearts. When you labor and are heavy laden, think of the melody that says, "Jesus took my burden and left me with a song." Peter reminded sufferers in the days of Nero to await their exaltation from God, "casting all your anxiety upon him, because he careth for you" (1 Peter 5:7).

The biggest burden for any person to bear is the burden of sin. The message of every part of the Bible is that Jesus bore that burden for us at Calvary. If He bore your heavy load of sin, He will not hesitate to help you carry every other conceivable load. Do you have a weight burdening your soul? Let our Lord lift it off your shoulders onto His.

He said He would be with you. Add any preposition to the promise, be it *on*, *across*, *in*, *through*, or whatever. He will be there from "on mountains" to "beneath heavy burdens." You can count on it. You have His promise.

3

Nothing New Under the Sun but Everything New Under the Son

Within
New Spirit
New Strength
New Song

Without
New Family
New Form
New Faith

Ahead
New Heaven
New House
New Hope

3

The Promise of Newness

The preacher is often misunderstood. I do not mean the one you listen to week by week. I refer to Solomon of old and to his work called "Ecclesiastes," or "The Preacher." Solomon is misunderstood. His work is misinterpreted.

His sermon begins, "Vanity of vanities, saith the Preacher; vanity of vanities, all is vanity" (Ecclesiastes 1:2). Solomon's message is said to be filled with pessimism, satiated with materialism, and loaded with fatalism. It cries out that life is empty, empty, empty. Just as waters come down from the heaven, flow into the rivers, run to the seas, and are lifted by sun's rays back into the sky again, so life goes on through inevitable cycles. You are born. You struggle. You die. Generation follows generation. Everything under the sun is empty and vain.

> Vanity of vanities, saith the Preacher; vanity of vanities, all is vanity. What profit hath man of all his labor wherein he laboreth under the sun? One generation goeth, and another generation cometh; but the earth abideth for ever. The sun also ariseth, and the sun goeth down, and hasteth to its place where it ariseth. The wind goeth toward the south, and turneth about unto the north; it turneth about continually in its course, and the wind returneth again to its circuits. All the rivers run

into the sea, yet the sea is not full; unto the place whither the rivers go, thither they go again. All things are full of weariness; man cannot utter it: the eye is not satisfied with seeing, nor the ear filled with hearing. That which hath been is that which shall be; and that which hath been done is that which shall be done: and there is no new thing under the sun. Is there a thing whereof it may be said, See, this is new? it hath been long ago, in the ages which were before us.

—Ecclesiastes 1:2-10

If ten verses of the sermon do not discourage you, ten chapters will. Try wine, women, and song; and life is still empty. Try wisdom, wealth, and worldly pleasure; and inner emptiness is still there.

Thirty-two times the preacher in the book of Ecclesiastes says some particular thing or everything is "vanity" or empty. But another preacher, Paul the apostle, assures us who are Christians that we have been buried with Christ through baptism and have risen to "walk in newness of life" (Romans 6:4).

Which preacher is right? Is Paul correct in saying there is new life in Jesus? Or is Solomon right in saying, "There is no new thing under the sun"? (Ecclesiastes 1:9).

Before you bring your verdict, hear my plea that the preacher Solomon is being misunderstood. What the wise Solomon actually is saying is this: When God is left out of man's life—when man forgets who reigns *above* the sun, when man just looks at life "*under* the sun" without the intervention of God—then life is meaningless.

Understand what Solomon is teaching. If you or I ignore the God who reigns above and look at life from the worldly point of view only, then everything is empty and vain. Preacher Paul believes what Solomon proclaimed. He does not contradict the old sermon. He too affirms how "vain" and "senseless" is the life of "fools" who ignore God (Romans 1:21, 22).

The key of Ecclesiastes is the phrase "under the sun." Solomon proclaims the vanity of life without God, but he ends his sermon by pointing beyond the sun: "Fear God, and keep his commandments; for this is the whole duty of man" (Ecclesiastes 12:13). Human effort can never find the secret of living life at its best. But thanks be to God, the Lord who sits above the heavens has intervened. He promised to do a "new thing" (Isaiah 43:19). He pledged to establish a "new covenant" (Hebrews 8:8-13; 12:24). He has revealed the way of a new life by a new birth (John 3:3-5).

The promise, in succinct and all-inclusive form, is well expressed in 2 Corinthians 5:17: "Wherefore if any man is in Christ, he is a new creature: the old things are passed away; behold, they are become new."

As we consider God's promise of newness, allow me to make a play on words. There is nothing new "under the sun," when the spelling is S-U-N, but there is something new "under the Son" when you write S-O-N, the Son of God.

Under the dominion of Jesus, the Son of God, everything becomes new, as promised. Things within become new. Things without become new. Things ahead of us become new.

Everything Within

Stepping out of darkness and coming under the dominion and radiance of Christ the Son, a person finds a new Spirit within. When the Holy Spirit descended on Pentecost and filled the apostles with His presence, they knew an uncontainable joy. Some accused them of being "filled with new wine" (Acts 2:13). But the apostles knew they were filled rather with a new Spirit—the Spirit of God (Acts 2:4, 33).

Jesus had taught that the "new wine" of the gospel would not be poured into the old wineskins of the law (Matthew 9:17). There is something too bubbly, too sparkling, too effervescent about the gospel to be contained under old forms.

The Holy Spirit touches people and fills them with life. The person born again is born both of the water and of the Spirit, as Jesus told Nicodemus (John 3:5). In the epistle to Titus the same truth is expressed in corresponding words: "He saved us, through the washing of regeneration and renewing of the Holy Spirit" (Titus 3:5). Those born again on Pentecost received "the gift of the Holy Spirit" upon their baptism (Acts 2:38) as do we (verse 39). It is God's divine presence within that brings power and assurance. Those buried with Christ "through baptism" have risen to "walk in newness of life" (Romans 6:4). That newness the Christian experiences is the result of the new Spirit within. He serves "in newness of the spirit, and not in oldness of the letter" (Romans 7:6).

Christians are counseled to avoid being filled "with wine," but to seek being "filled with the Spirit" (Ephesians 5:18). Those who are filled with the spirits of alcohol are changed. They speak like drunken people, reel as in a stupor, and act intoxicated. Those whose lives are taken over by God's Spirit are changed too. They talk, walk, and act differently. But what a difference! Instead of falling under the influence of wine, God's people stand erect in the presence of sin because they are "under the influence" of the Spirit of God. Once a man has within him the new Spirit, he senses a new strength. He finds the words of Isaiah to be true: "They that wait for Jehovah shall renew their strength; they shall mount up with wings as eagles; they shall run, and not be weary; they shall walk, and not faint" (Isaiah 40:31). Such a person makes David's words his own: "Jehovah is my light and my salvation; whom shall I fear? Jehovah is the strength of my life; of whom shall I be afraid?" (Psalm 27:1).

The preacher, Solomon, was right in saying that "under the sun" there is nothing new. The preacher, Paul, was right in proclaiming that if a life is lived "under the Son" of God, everything has become new. Under Christ there is a new Spirit. Under God's Son there is a new strength within. Under the Lord Jesus there is a new song in the heart. Delivered from the pit of iniquity we sing our personal testimony: "He brought me up also out of a horrible pit, out of the miry clay; and he set my feet upon a rock, and established my goings. And he hath put a new song in my mouth, even praise unto our God" (Psalm 40:2, 3).

Leave God out of your life and, as Solomon said, there will be "nothing new under the sun." But place Christ over your life and there will be a new Spirit, a new strength, and a new song within.

Everything Without

"If any man is in Christ, he is a new creature: the old things are passed away; behold, they are become new" (2 Corinthians 5:17). Everything within has become new. Everything without becomes new, different, superior, unusual. The promises say so. In addition, experience informs us that the change God works in life has to do with the exterior as well as the interior. I remember accepting Christ as my Savior many years ago. It was evident immediately that I had become a part of a family. Think of the time of your conversion. Do you remember how arms of brothers and sisters in Christ reached out to take you in? You were now a part of the church local and the church universal. Instantly you belonged to all Christians of all time. You had family in this world and in the world to come.

When a child is born, he wears the last name of his parents. This custom is ancient and widespread. *Simon Bar-Jonah* means *Simon son of John* (or *Jonah*). *MacDougal* means *son of Dougal; Peterson* indicates *son of Peter; Ben Ezra* is *son of Ezra*. Our name *Christian* (Acts 11:26) has a meaning as well. It links us not only with Christ, but also with God the Father, for Jesus is "the Christ of God" (Luke 9:20). The word *Christian* tells the world to whom we belong. We are in the family of God and His Son, Jesus Christ. In that name we bring glory to them (1 Peter 4:16). Sectarian names will not suffice. *Christian* is the name we use when we speak of all God's children redeemed through Christ.

This new family with its new name worships the Heavenly Father under new forms. When John's disciples observed that Christ did not fast as the Pharisees did, Jesus explained that it is inappropriate to put new patches on old garments or new wine in old wineskins (Matthew 9:14-17). Christianity has a newness about it. The Old Covenant ways, fitted to Judaism, are not to be the forms for worship in the church.

The "sabbath day" was the weekly holy day under the Mosaic law (Exodus 20:8-11). The "Lord's day" (Revelation 1:10), "the first day of the week," is the day of Christ's resurrection (Mark 16:9). This is the day when Christ's disciples gather "to break bread" (Acts 20:7) and the day of pooling resources into God's treasury (1 Corinthians 16:2).

Old Israel for many centuries has gathered in synagogues and read from the Torah and the prophets. New Israel, the church, assembles in a variety of places, and their reading includes writings of Christ's apostles and their associates as well as the older Scriptures. A significant new activity marking the Christian assembly is the observance of the Lord's Supper. These new forms express the new gospel of Christ's death and resurrection. The new rites symbolize our new faith.

On Mar's Hill in Athens, the philosophers asked Paul, "May we know what this new teaching is, which is spoken by thee?" (Acts 17:19). They always liked "to tell or to hear some new thing" (verse 21). When Luke records this, he is paying no compliment to the Athenians in their unending search for new human philosophies. In Christianity there is a genuine and lasting newness that takes away every need to search for something else new.

The old law was temporary. The gospel is permanent. The law given at the exodus, "four hundred and thirty years" after the promise to Abraham, was "added" only "till the seed should come to whom the promise hath been made" (Galatians 3:17-19). That law served as a "tutor to bring us unto Christ, that we might be justified by faith. But now that faith is come, we are no longer under a tutor" (Galatians 3:24, 25).

Not ascending Sinai as Moses did, but ascending a mountain in Galilee, Jesus contrasted himself to Moses the old lawgiver. He who established the new kingdom with its new laws spoke with authority: "Ye have heard that it was said to them of old time, Thou shalt not kill . . . but I say unto you, that every one who is angry with his brother shall be in danger of the judgment" (Matthew 5:21, 22). Six times Jesus quoted what was said on tables of stone or written in Moses' writings, and with that He contrasted His higher demands for the new age. The new faith was not leaving a high road for a low road. It was going from the highest ethical code known to man to the new regime of God, which reveals a way even higher.

The disciples of Christ were not sent out to repeat the message that Israelites had given since Moses' day. They were to herald from the housetops a new and renewing faith. Their commission was to teach men "to observe all things whatsoever I [Christ] commanded you" (Matthew 28:20). It was not to reiterate what Moses commanded Israel.

Everything Ahead

In Christ everything becomes new—that which is within, that which is without, and that which is ahead. Things were changed internally, externally, and eternally. Solomon's "there is no new thing under the sun" (Ecclesiastes 1:9) describes the vanity of life without God's intervention. Christians know that God has broken into history in the coming of Jesus. They are certain that all who live "under the Son"—God's Son, Jesus—will find all things new.

Isaiah spoke of "the new heavens and the new earth" that would be coming one day far ahead in the future (Isaiah 66:22). John wrote centuries later of the same "new heaven and new earth" that still lay ahead for God's people (Revelation 21:1). By eyes of faith he saw the eternal tomorrow with God tabernacling with men and drying all human tears. The voice from the throne assured those who had walked by faith throughout time that the promise of newness ahead was now fulfilled. He speaks: "Behold, I make all things new." Can that promise be as certain as God's other promises have proved to be? The confident voice thunders from the throne: "Write: for these words are faithful and true" (Revelation 21:2-5).

Some day this world will be destroyed with fire as Noah's age perished by water. Peter will not let his readers forget either the destruction of long ago or the destruction to come. He begs them,

> Seeing that these things are thus all to be dissolved, what manner of persons ought ye to be in all holy living and godliness, looking for and earnestly desiring the coming of the day of God, by reason of which the heavens being on fire shall be dissolved, and the elements shall melt with fervent heat? But, according to his promise, we look for new heavens and a new earth, wherein dwelleth righteousness.
> —2 Peter 3:11-13

In our present world much sin and unrighteousness dwell. Hardly a day goes by but the headlines tell of another murder, another case of arson, another rape, another robbery. It is a lifting fact that in the "new heavens" things are going to be both new and different.

In the promises of God, along with the new heaven comes a new house in which we will dwell. Your aches and pains may already be hinting to you that the Bible is right when it speaks of the "outward man . . . decaying" at the same time the "inward man is renewed day by day" (2 Corinthians 4:16). What can we know about our future body? Paul continues: "For we know that if the earthly house of our tabernacle be dissolved, we have a building from God, a house not made with hands, eternal, in the heavens. For verily in this we groan, longing to be clothed upon with our habitation which is from heaven" (2 Corinthians 5:1, 2).

In the new world we get a new house. This old house groans along with all creation (Romans 8:22, 23). This old body knows pain and suffering. But our future dwelling place is not built for time. It is built for eternity. It will not get old, decrepit, or weak. It will go on forever.

Christian faith is right in looking ahead to tomorrow and not living only for today. "If we have only hoped in Christ in this life, we are of all men most pitiable" (1 Corinthians 15:19). We live by the promise that this body "sown in corruption" will be "raised in incorruption." What is "sown in dishonor" and "weakness" will be raised in "glory" and "power" (1 Corinthians 15:42, 43).

When bodily aches and pains come in knees and shoulders, arms and hands, backs and legs, we may be tempted to sound like Ecclesiastes. We may feel the pessimism of those Solomon described as living "under the sun," without God, where "all is vanity." Sometimes life can be miserable. But Christ came. That means new hope. That means after darkness comes dawn.

First Thessalonians 4:13 reads, "But we would not have you ignorant, brethren, concerning them that fall asleep; that ye sorrow not, even as the rest, who have no hope." These are the options: "no hope" out of Christ, or new hope in Christ. Live life "under the sun," ignore God's will and plans for human life, seek to make it all on your own; then all is vanity and there is no hope.

But there is an altogether different way. Live your life "under the Son," who loved you and gave himself up for you. Live under the one who came to earth from above the stars. Live under the new covenant confirmed by His blood. Then instead of "no hope" there is "new hope."

Is it any wonder the gospel has such attraction to mortal men? In Jesus, life takes on newness—within, without, and ahead. What does the world have to offer? If atheism, agnosticism, and humanism are all there is, life is vain. But from Solomon's day to John the revelator's day and on to our day and beyond, God exists and God cares and God has come into history. Therefore men "under the Son" have reason to hope. As J. D. Murch sings,

> The world all about me has now no allure:
>   Its pleasures bring pain,
>   Its wisdom is vain;
> I seek a foundation that's steadfast and sure.
>   I'll put Jesus first in my life.

Will you? Be *new* and be new *now*.

4

JOY

of Christmas
of Consummation
of Conversion

4

The Promise of Joy

Our gracious friends constantly wish us joy. They say "Have a nice day." They greet us with "Happy Anniversary" or "Happy Holiday." Near the end of a year their wish is "Merry Christmas." A few days later their greeting has become "Happy New Year." Sometimes a group prepares a cake with candles and they salute in unison: "Many happy returns of the day of thy birth."

Is this human desire for our happiness also Heaven's desire? Does God wish us well? Does He want us to know joy? What is His will regarding human happiness?

Listen to answers from the Bible. "Rejoice always; pray without ceasing; in everything give thanks: for this is the will of God in Christ Jesus to you-ward" (1 Thessalonians 5:16-18). Hear Nehemiah's assurance: "The joy of Jehovah is your strength" (Nehemiah 8:10). Give ear to the call of the psalmist: "Make a joyful noise unto Jehovah, all ye lands. Serve Jehovah with gladness: come before his presence with singing" (Psalm 100:1, 2). "Rejoice in the Lord always: again I will say, Rejoice," writes Paul (Philippians 4:4). He reminds the Galatians that "the fruit of the Spirit is . . . joy" (Galatians 5:22). To the Romans he declares, "The kingdom of God is . . . righteousness and peace and joy in the Holy Spirit" (Romans 14:17). Peter says that Christians "greatly rejoice, though now for a little while . . . ye have been put to grief in manifold trials." He speaks of Jesus, "whom not having seen ye love; on whom, though now ye see him not, yet believing, ye rejoice greatly with joy unspeakable and full of glory" (1 Peter 1:6-8).

From one end of sacred writings to the other there is the command to rejoice, rejoice, rejoice. But thorough investigation of Bible texts shows more than *commanded* joy. It reveals *promised* joy. It will be to our eternal benefit to learn where that promised happiness is to be found.

The Joy of Christmas

From the Old Testament's first promise of a coming Messiah to its last, we find God planting the joy of anticipation in human hearts. What gladness fills the air when we remember the advent of our Lord! What happiness floods the soul when we think of the wonder of incarnation—that God came to live among us and bring redemption! The Christmas season in the church's calendar focuses on the love of God that sent Christ to be with us. At the thought of that event joy abounds.

We carol, "Joy to the world! the Lord is come; let earth receive her King." We invite others to join in the glad refrain: "O come, all ye faithful, joyful and triumphant. . . . O come, let us adore Him, Christ, the Lord."

Jesus' coming put music in the heart. It set human lips to singing. Every carol radiates the joy—the long-promised joy—that God foretold from ages past.

The Gospels of Matthew and Luke give accounts of Jesus' birth. Since the word *gospel* means good news, it is no surprise when a written Gospel begins with the joyous tidings of the birth of God's Son.

Luke tells of shepherds in the Bethlehem country hearing angels announce, "Be not afraid; for behold, I bring you good tidings of great joy which shall be to all the people: for there is born to you this day in the city of David a Saviour, who is Christ the Lord" (Luke 2:10, 11). Matthew reports that Wise-men from the distant East were guided to the very house where the young child was. He describes their excitement with these words: "And when they saw the star, they rejoiced with exceeding great joy" (Matthew 2:10).

A few months before this happy, blessed event, Mary and Elizabeth were together. Elizabeth was pregnant with John the Baptist and she described what happened when Mary arrived. She said,

"When the voice of thy salutation came into mine ears, the babe leaped in my womb for joy" (Luke 1:44). Mary responded in words of praise to God: "My soul doth magnify the Lord, and my spirit hath rejoiced in God my Saviour" (verses 46, 47).

The carols celebrating the nativity are joyous because the Bible references to the event are full of gladness. The New Testament accounts of the birth reflect unparalleled joy, but what about the ancient promises that we call prophecies? Jesus spoke to that question in John 8:56. He said to the Jews, "Your father Abraham rejoiced to see my day; and he saw it, and was glad." The source of Abraham's gladness was the promise God made to him along with a life-changing command:

> Get thee out of thy country, and from thy kindred, and from thy father's house, unto the land that I will show thee: and I will make of thee a great nation, and I will bless thee, and make thy name great; and be thou a blessing: and I will bless them that bless thee, and him that curseth thee will I curse: and in thee shall all the families of the earth be blessed.
> —Genesis 12:1-3

Abraham did personally bring blessings to many, but the greater blessing was promised through his seed, his descendant (Genesis 22:18). That greater blessing came through Christ, the promised seed of Abraham (Galatians 3:16). Isaiah foresaw that glad day and predicted, "A virgin shall conceive, and bear a son, and shall call his name Immanuel"—God with us (Isaiah 7:14). The prophet further filled hearts with joy when he announced, "Unto us a child is born, unto us a son is given; and the government shall be upon his shoulder: and his name shall be called Wonderful, Counsellor, Mighty God, Everlasting Father, Prince of Peace" (Isaiah 9:6). When other prophets spoke of the coming one, their announcements too had the sound of joy. God was sending His Messiah to redeem the world. Such good news revealed long ago must not be silenced in any period of mankind's earthly stay.

"Joy to the world" indeed! The fact that God became man is great beyond compare. It brings joy unmatched. Therefore we must guard against letting *fable* take center stage where the revealed *fact* belongs. Whatever place you choose to give to Santa Claus and make-believe, be certain that you, your children, and your friends hear the greatest story every told.

Often we hear the slogan, "Keep Christ in Christmas." That is good. Commercialism, alcoholism, and both hubbub and humbug can hide the grandest of realities. If we let them take control, the Christ of Christmas can be forgotten in the excitement of snow and make-believe of a sleigh coming from the North Pole. Joseph Clark reminds us with these verses:

> The birthday of our Lord draws near:
> The Day of Days of all the year:
> A day of hope and joy and cheer.
>   Keep Jesus Christ in Christmas.
>
> Let no old Santa crowd Him out
> With whiskers grey and body stout.
> He helps the world forget about
>   The loving Christ at Christmas.
>
> The day is Christ's by right divine,
> A day no myth should undermine,
> A day when thoughts and deeds sublime
>   Should keep the Christ in Christmas.
>
> When every message, every gift,
> Should in some joyous way uplift
> One's very thoughts, and make them drift
>   To Bethlehem at Christmas,
>
> Give other things a minor place,
> But tell to men of every race
> The story of this day of grace—
>   Of Christ, their Lord on Christmas.

No fiction can match the fact. The divine Creator took the form of a man and came to live awhile on earth. The Lord of life accepted death to redeem us, to make it possible for us to live forever in Heaven. Because of what He did for us, we have passed out of death into life (John 5:24).

If you seek to know where joy is promised in the Bible, you read Old Testament prophecies and they point to Christ's coming. You read New Testament records and they report the joy that accompanied His advent. It matters little whether He came in December or

June or some other month. The time of His coming was a time of joy, and any month of the year is a good time to think of His coming and renew our joy.

The Joy of Consummation

Ancient saints looked forward to the joy of Christ's first coming, and with like anticipation we now look forward to His second coming. At the Lord's return we shall experience the joy of consummation, the completion of earthly history.

I never tire of telling about the little girl who pressed her nose against the pet-shop window. Her father enjoyed looking at his daughter more that at the puppies that had caught her eye. He could not resist buying her the pet dog of her choosing. She looked them all over, especially the one closest to her that was wagging his tail with glee. "Which one do you want, honey?" asked the Daddy. She replied, "I want the one with the happy ending!"

At the consummation of history, for every Christian there will be a happy ending. When you read a murder mystery, do you read the last chapter first, so you will know how it is going to turn out? It is not a bad idea at all to go to the last book of the Bible and its last chapters. The struggles of life are easier to handle when you know how things will turn out at the end. When frightening things happen today and you see the mess the world is in, you are grateful that God placed at the end of His Book the happy ending that awaits His people.

John describes the beauty of the new heaven and the new earth with the holy city, new Jerusalem (Revelation 21). He declares that when the seventh and last angel sounded his trumpet, great voices in Heaven joined in announcing total victory for righteousness. They cried, "The kingdom of the world is become the kingdom of our Lord, and of his Christ: and he shall reign for ever and ever" (Revelation 11:15).

At this consummation, the call goes out for gladness in every heart: "Let us rejoice and be exceeding glad, and let us give the glory unto him: for the marriage of the Lamb is come" (Revelation 19:7). In that glad day it is promised that "God shall wipe away every tear from their eyes" (Revelation 7:17).

To add to our joy, we shall see Jesus "even as he is" (1 John 3:2). Considering this "blissful moment," Mrs. Frank A. Breck was prompted to write these lines:

> Face to face with Christ my Saviour,
>   Face to face—what will it be
> When with rapture I behold Him,
>   Jesus Christ who died for me?
>
> Face to face I shall behold Him,
>   Far beyond the starry sky;
> Face to face in all His glory,
>   I shall see Him by and by!

We will find our joy of seeing Jesus enhanced by seeing many Christian friends. In both Thessalonian letters Paul gives a tremendous amount of information regarding Christ's second coming. The apostle puts his finger on one cause of his anticipated happiness when time ends. He asks, "For what is our hope, or joy, or crown of glorying? Are not even ye, before our Lord Jesus at his coming? For ye are our glory and our joy" (1 Thessalonians 2:19, 20). Many miles of space and many years of time might separate Paul from the converts he made across the world; but the day was coming when he would enjoy seeing them again at the resurrection.

On some future day we shall see every hospital bed empty, every rest-home room vacated, and every grave giving up its dead. All our Christian loved ones, in restored health and vigor, will be with Jesus. What joy it will be to tour Heaven with these friends! Since no tourist can see even Rome or Athens in a single day, the resurrected saints will need eternity to see the new heavens and the new earth (2 Peter 3:13); and we will have forever.

As we walk the streets of new Jerusalem, every step of the way we shall sense the fulfillment of Christ's promise spoken long ago: "Rejoice, and be exceeding glad: for great is your reward in heaven" (Matthew 5:12). We shall hear, "Well done, good and faithful servant," and we shall "enter . . . into the joy" of the Lord (Matthew 25:21). Today, as we anticipate the end, "we rejoice in hope of the glory of God" (Romans 5:2). Even though death may seem to win a victory, we stand by the tomb with the promise of Christ's return in our minds. We can believe with David, "Weeping may tarry for the night, but joy cometh in the morning" (Psalm 30:5). Though we are "put to grief in manifold trials," we believe in Jesus and love Him; and therefore we "rejoice greatly with joy unspeakable and full of glory" because we are sure of the salvation of our souls and the souls of our loved ones (1 Peter 1:6-8).

The Joy of Conversion

God promised joy to the world, and so He gave us His Son. God promises joy to the saved at the consummation of history, and that joy will come. But between the promised joy of Christ's first coming and the promised delights of His second coming, lies another promise of joy. This joy is basic to our future. Should we miss this one, the other joys will fade away. I speak of the promised joy that comes to us at conversion. Read these lines from an unknown writer:

> 'Tis not enough that Christ was born
>   Beneath the star that shone,
> And earth was set that happy morn
>   Within the golden zone.
> He must be born within the heart
>   Before He finds His throne
> And brings the day of love and good,
> The reign of Christ-like brotherhood.

The book of Acts is called the book of conversions. It not only tells that the apostles carried the gospel beyond the borders of Palestine, but also reports with what joy the gospel was received in each new territory. Read these summary verses that tell how the work of Christ grew as the gospel spread to new communities: Acts 6:7; 9:31; 12:24; 16:5; 19:20; and 28:30, 31. We might call these "victory verses," or even "happy endings." Where the story of the cross was accepted, joy filled the area.

Bible students search the different cases of conversion to see how people became Christians. We should never tire of reviewing the facts and seeing that all converts of Bible times came to faith, repentance, and baptism. This is true whether they were Jerusalemites, Samaritans, Ethiopians, or Europeans.

But consider again those records of people who came to faith. This time, look beyond their acts of response to the descriptions of their joy at obedience.

The converts of Pentecost "day by day . . . took their food with gladness and singleness of heart" (Acts 2:46). Happiness was there because forgiveness was there and the Holy Spirit dwelt within.

When Philip presented the gospel in Samaria and "the multitudes gave heed with one accord," Luke relates that "there was much joy in that city" (Acts 8:5-8).

Philip buried in the waters of baptism a man of Ethiopia who served the queen, Candace. The newborn Christian rose out of the water. Notice Luke's choice of words here: "And the eunuch saw him [Philip] no more, for he went on his way rejoicing" (Acts 8:39).

When Saul saw Christ on the Damascus Road, his guilt for past actions drove him to his knees. After three heavy-laden days without food (Acts 9:9), Saul found the burden lifted in his obedience to the baptismal command. The record adds, "And he took food and was strengthened" (Acts 9:19). His guilt was gone, his appetite returned, and despair was replaced with joy. His happiness is reflected in the words he wrote much later: "I count all things to be loss for the excellency of the knowledge of Christ Jesus my Lord" (Philippians 3:8).

Similarly, when the jailor's household was baptized at Philippi, what followed was celebration and a happy meal because there was joy to share. Luke writes,

> And he [the jailor] took them the same hour of the night, and washed their stripes; and was baptized, he and all his, immediately. And he brought them up into his house, and set food before them, and rejoiced greatly, with all his house, having believed in God.
> —Acts 16:33, 34

Having heard this testimony of how joy follows conversion in the Acts record, tune your ears now to the testimony in the Gospel record.

To a paralytic one day Jesus said, "Son, be of good cheer; thy sins are forgiven" (Matthew 9:2). There can be nothing but joy within when a life finds the remission of sins.

Since Jesus as the Messiah was about to establish God's kingdom, He clarified the nature of that kingdom. One way He did so was by preaching the Sermon on the Mount. You remember that famous speech began with what we call the Beatitudes (Matthew 5:3-12). Every line of those opening words of the mountaintop message started with the word *blessed*. Jesus announced the good news: "Blessed are the poor in spirit. . . . Blessed are they that mourn. . . . Blessed are the meek." You remember the Beatitudes, but do you remember that the oft-repeated word *blessed* means joyous or happy? Happy is the man who feels so poor in spiritual things that he will accept a Savior. Happy is the man who will shed a penitent tear for sins committed and will find the comfort of forgiveness. Happy are those who hunger and thirst for a righteousness that they cannot obtain for themselves, but that God offers as a gift. Recipients of such grace shall be filled.

Jesus often taught in parables. Finding God's kingdom, said the master story-teller, is like finding a treasure in a field. A man unexpectedly runs into the treasure of the gospel, and "in his joy he goeth and selleth all that he hath, and buyeth that field" (Matthew 13:44). Some people find truth accidentally, as the thief on the cross may have done (Luke 23:39-43). But others search for it, as did the Ethiopian (Acts 8:27-34) and Cornelius (Acts 10:1-6). Therefore Jesus added the parable of the merchant searching for the goodly pearl. His joy is revealed by his willingness to pay any price for the supreme pearl (Matthew 13:45, 46). Wherever one finds the treasure Christ offers, there is joy.

Thus in plain records, in Beatitudes, and in parables, the Gospels show that God promises joy at conversion. That becomes plainer yet in three stories about the finding of lost things. These are told in Luke, chapter 15.

A shepherd finds a sheep that strayed, and "layeth it on his shoulders, rejoicing." But the good news is too great to keep to himself. "He calleth together his friends and his neighbors, saying unto them, Rejoice with me, for I have found my sheep which was lost." Lest any listener miss the application and think only of sheep, Jesus interpreted the meaning: "I say unto you, that even so there shall be joy in heaven over one sinner that repenteth" (Luke 15:3-7).

A woman searches her home for a coin she has lost. She has no intention of stopping the search "until she find it." When at last the lost is found, she too invites friends to the celebration: "Rejoice with me, for I have found the piece which I had lost." Jesus wants the hearer of the story to know "There is joy in the presence of the angels of God over one sinner that repenteth" (Luke 15:8-10).

The third story of that day tells of the prodigal son who comes home to his waiting father. The elder brother expresses total dissatisfaction with the joyous reception the father gives, a reception with feasting, celebration, music, and dancing. The father represents God; the older son represents the Pharisees who criticized Jesus for associating with sinners. (Does he represent some of us? Are we dismayed when a really vile sinner comes to God and His church?) Hear the father's tender explanation: "It was meet to make merry and be glad: for this thy brother was dead, and is alive again; and was lost, and is found" (Luke 15:32). Jesus, who knows what Heaven is like, says that every conversion fills Heaven with happiness.

A nun is reported to have said, "All the way to heaven is heaven." I like that. She knew the joy God promised. A Scotsman, I am told, explained, "I am happier now when I'm not happy, than I used to be when I was happy." He knew the joy God promised. Colonel Sanders, who made world-famous his "finger-licken-good" chicken, requested that at his death Pat Boone should be asked to sing: "He touched me, and oh the joy that floods my soul." He experienced the joy promised at the new birth. He could have requested any number of hymns that tell the same fact of joy in being saved: "O happy day that fixed my choice" or "Ring the bells of heaven! there is joy today, for a soul returning from the wild."

Since Jesus came the first time, joy has been available. When Jesus returns again, there will be gladness for the redeemed. At the moment when Christ is received as Savior, the promised joy of salvation becomes the personal possession of another baptized believer. As in apostolic days, disciples are "filled with joy and with the Holy Spirit" (Acts 13:52). Thank God for another promise from on high. Thank God for the promise of joy.

5

Healing Is

in the atonement
at the adoption
for the acquitted

5

The Promise of Healing

To understand God's promise of healing, we need to read Romans 8 with care. Some consider it to be the greatest chapter in the Bible. It starts great, finishes great, and is great in its heart. It is that center or heart that speaks to the promise of healing.

Romans 8 begins with this magnificent declaration from the pen of the inspired apostle:

> There is therefore now no condemnation to them that are in Christ Jesus. For the law of the Spirit of life in Christ Jesus made me free from the law of sin and of death.
> —Romans 8:1, 2

The glorious doxology that concludes the chapter reemphasizes the assurance of the opening verses:

> We are more than conquerors through him that loved us. For I am persuaded, that neither death, nor life, nor angels, nor principalities, nor things present, nor things to come, nor powers, nor height, nor depth, nor any other creature, shall be able to separate us from the love of God, which is in Christ Jesus our Lord.
> —Romans 8:37-39

Now in the heart and core of this great chapter of Romans, between its great opening and great closing, is discussed man's great problem. The topic is pain. The question raised is the dilemma of suffering and sickness.

Sample what is written. Paul reminds his readers that we are "joint-heirs with Christ; if so be that we suffer with him." He admonishes them, "I reckon that the sufferings of this present time are not worthy to be compared with the glory which shall be revealed" (Romans 8:17, 18). He indicates that all creation is eagerly waiting for the time when we will be glorified, for along with us the whole creation will be delivered from "vanity" and "the bondage of corruption" (Romans 8:19-21). Then he turns on the light of understanding in these words we especially want to consider:

> For we know that the whole creation groaneth and travaileth in pain together until now. And not only so, but ourselves also, who have the first-fruits of the Spirit, even we ourselves groan within ourselves, waiting for our adoption, to wit, the redemption of our body. For in hope were we saved: but hope that is seen is not hope: for who hopeth for that which he seeth? But if we hope for that which we see not, then do we with patience wait for it.
>
> —Romans 8:22-25

That sounds like the Christian in the present life is to experience bodily pain. Can we suppose then that God will never allow His faithful people to be sick?

Wrestle first with this question: "Is there physical healing in the atonement?" Almost any Saturday in the religious section of a major newspaper you will find advertisements inviting people to a "healing meeting." Some invitations remind the reader to seek bodily healing because such healing for today is "in the atonement." Anyone coming to Christ can today find forgiveness in calling on Christ. Just as certainly, it is reasoned, anyone asking for healing can find instant and total wholeness today because that too is included in that atonement made at Calvary.

Is there physical healing in the atonement? Our question is not "Does God care and answer prayer when we suffer aches or pains or sickness?" Of course God cares. "His heart is touched with my grief." Certainly He hears us when we pray. The question is not "Does God care?" nor is it "Is the Christian way of life the healthiest way to live?" Proper attitudes and clean habits do contribute to better physical health.

The precise question is "Is there physical healing in the atonement?" I could wish to answer the inquiry affirmatively. Walking almost daily through hospital rooms and rest-home corridors, I have wished often that these who suffer could be vigorous and youthful and healthy once again. When I receive some doctor's bill for a physical exam or the hospital's statement for a week in the three-bed ward, I could hope for a divine way of escape. But in my wishing I must not mistake my will for God's wiser will. And I must search the Word of God lest I offer false hopes for real hopes. False hopes are worse than no hopes at all.

We have the question before us then. Let us search now for the answer.

Healing Is in the Atonement

One thing we know for sure is that the Bible records healing even before the atonement, before Jesus died on the cross. In Old Testament story we can read that God intervened to heal before Christ came. When Jesus came, as the Gospels record, He was found to be not only the Master Teacher and the Good Shepherd; He was heralded as the Great Physician.

It was before Jesus' atoning death that He worked many miracles of healing. These established His deity (see John 20:30, 31), and served as object lessons of His mission to heal sinners from their dread disease of sin. As Paul showed appreciation for Doctor Luke by terming him "the beloved physician" (Colossians 4:14), Jesus compared the sinner's need for a Savior to the sick man's need for a doctor. His familiar words were, "They that are whole have no need of a physician, but they that are sick" (Matthew 9:12).

As we view Jesus' healing ministry through the eyes of the Gospel writers, we thrill at His love and power. Blind men see, lame men walk, lepers are clean again, dumb lips speak. The Jesus of New Testament record cared for people that were hurting and used His almighty power to free them from their misery and pain. Isaiah had foreseen Christ's ministry, His healings, and His death: "Himself took our infirmities, and bare our diseases" (Isaiah 53:4 quoted in Matthew 8:17).

The apostles saw their Master do unquestionably genuine miracles. His healings were real, instant, complete, and lasting. No one was turned away. He healed them all. He created hope. Like the other Gospel writers, Mark records that people with various sicknesses were "made whole" (Mark 6:56). At the end of his account, having shown Christ's power over every distress in which man finds himself, Mark records the promise that "he that believeth and is baptized shall be saved" (Mark 16:16). The word *saved* is the same term that is translated *made whole* to record the deliverance Jesus brought by His healing miracles. This word means either saved from sickness or saved from eternal damnation. May we not conclude that each physical healing is to be viewed as a demonstration of the power to do the greatest healing of all—the miracle of salvation?

But back to our question: Is physical healing in the atonement? Healing from sin is certainly in that atonement. Isaiah 53:4-6 reads,

> Surely he hath borne our griefs, and carried our sorrows; yet we did esteem him stricken, smitten of God, and afflicted. But he was wounded for our transgressions, he was bruised for our iniquities; the chastisement of our peace was upon him; and with his stripes we are healed. All we like sheep have gone astray; we have turned every one to his own way; and Jehovah hath laid on him the iniquity of us all.

Clearly this foretells salvation from sin: "our transgressions" and "our iniquities." But how shall we understand "we are healed"? Does this mean all our physical illnesses are cured?

How did the inspired apostles understand Isaiah's words? We turn to Peter's use of the passage "with his stripes we are healed." How did this man, who sat at Jesus' feet for special training, understand this healing passage?

Hear Peter's quotation of the promise of healing in its context. Speaking of Christ, Peter says,

> His own self bare our sins in his body upon the tree, that we, having died unto sins, might live unto righteousness; by whose stripes ye were healed. For ye were going astray like sheep; but are now returned unto the Shepherd and Bishop of your souls.
>
> —1 Peter 2:24, 25

The apostle's use of the Isaiah 53 passage indicates that our healing is a rescue from "sins," a restoration to "righteousness," a returning from straying to following the "Shepherd" of our souls. The healing is a healing from sin rather than from sickness.

Nevertheless, I can agree that the healing in the atonement includes physical healing. At the end of time, everything lost through sin will be recovered because of the atonement. Paradise lost will at Christ's return be Paradise regained.

The ultimate cause of disease and pain is sin, as Genesis 3 shows. Since sin, the cause of physical evil, finds its cure in the cross, the consequences of sin also will go from us. But when? As we search the Scripture for the answer to that pertinent question, keep in mind that we are not called upon in the Scripture to repent of sickness or of death, but of sin. All sin in our lives is to stop now. Sickness will cease later.

Healing Is at the Adoption

We need to return to what God says through Paul in Romans 8. He speaks of our hoping for what Christians do not yet experience in this life. He dates that full healing, "the redemption of our body," at our "adoption" (Romans 8:23, 24), which occurs at the second coming of Christ.

But before we hear the "thus saith the Lord" of Scripture, let us listen to "thus saith common sense" and "thus say hard, cold facts." What saith common sense?

What was lost by man when he sinned was life itself. "The wages of sin is death" (Romans 6:23). Even though Christ centuries ago in His atonement paid the debt for me, yet I must one day join the whole race of man in dying. All the Christians of the last two thousand years have known or will know the experience of "passing away." Oh yes, some will still be living when Jesus comes. But with those exceptions, Christians as well as sinners experience physical death.

If believers have to wait until resurrection day to receive immortal bodies, it seems logical to expect their complete health and restoration of perfect soundness at the same time death itself is overcome. Since sin brought in sickness, pain, and death together, why should we expect total deliverance from one before deliverance from the others? Thus saith common sense.

What say cold statistics and hard facts? I know scores of sincere believers who hold that, since divine healing is in the atonement, with faith they will never know sickness. I live in Fullerton, California, and almost daily pass a Christian Science Rest Home. Sin, sickness, and death to these dear people may be but an "error of mortal mind." Yet, like their neighbors, they find that their bodies age, weaken, go through a process of decay, and die (see 2 Corinthians 4:16).

Some of my finest friends in the Christian ministry classify themselves as "Pentecostals." They disagree with my understanding of God's healing today. Yet one hard, cold fact is evident. Their busy schedules are much like mine. Their parishioners need to be visited in rest homes. There are hospital calls they too must make. They too have funerals to conduct in their weekly agendas.

I doubt seriously that a scientific testing would find much difference in the percentage of "charismatics" and "non-charismatics" having filled teeth, wearing corrective lenses, and experiencing loss of hair. Even Oral Roberts has built his magnificent hospital because Christians of all persuasions find that sickness is not miraculously overcome in this "vale of tears."

But your mind is not on asking preachers and teachers, "What saith common sense?" or "What say cold statistics?" You want to know, and I want to know, "What say the Christian Scriptures?" Do they lead us to look for miraculous healing of all our bodily ills now?

We are back to Romans 8. It says we are saved in hope. Paul argues that "hope that is seen is not hope: for who hopeth for that which he seeth? But if we hope for that which we see not, then do we with patience wait for it" (Romans 8:24, 25). This means there is a dimension to our salvation that is future and is not a part of the present.

The apostle says, "The whole creation groaneth and travaileth in pain together until now" (Romans 8:22). Not long before Paul wrote these words to the Romans, he shared with the Corinthians the thought that "though our outward man is decaying, yet our inward man is renewed day by day" (2 Corinthians 4:16).

What God's people now have is "the first-fruits of the Spirit" (Romans 8:23). As earnest money is accepted as a guarantee of full payment later, we have the Spirit as a guarantee of more to follow (2 Corinthians 5:5). "Sight" is for tomorrow. We have now a promise from God. We can rest on that.

The Philippian letter was written after Paul was imprisoned for two years in Caesarea and while he was a prisoner in Rome. It was written after Epaphroditus' bout with a sickness "nigh unto death"

(Philippians 2:25-27). In that letter the apostle told of waiting for the return of the Lord, "who shall fashion anew the body of our humiliation" (Philippians 3:21).

Paul knew humiliation of the body. He was buffeted by "a thorn in the flesh" (2 Corinthians 12:7). He admonished his son in the gospel to avoid contaminated water and "use a little wine" for his "stomach's sake" and his "often infirmities" (1 Timothy 5:23). With all his sincere faith and constant service, Timothy knew sickness often. Another co-worker, Trophimus, once had to be left behind because he was sick (2 Timothy 4:20).

This should be no surprise to us. Jesus said our eternal destiny depends in part on our visiting Him when He is sick: that is, on our visiting His "brethren" in their sickness (Matthew 25:34-40). Does this not suggest that all through the gospel age Christ's people will experience sickness as well as hunger, thirst, and nakedness?

Today, in the present world, we are brothers and partakers in tribulation (Revelation 1:9). Tomorrow, in the new world, at the resurrection of our transformed bodies, we will experience all that Christ's atonement purchased. Tomorrow is the day of redemption for which we are sealed by the Holy Spirit of God (Ephesians 4:30). Tomorrow is the "new heaven and the new earth" (Revelation 21:1). Tomorrow we shall "hunger no more . . . and God shall wipe away every tear" (Revelation 7:16, 17).

At Jesus' return from Heaven we are going to have new bodies. The body we bury will change at the resurrection. It is sown in "corruption . . . dishonor . . . weakness." It will be raised in "incorruption . . . glory . . . power" (1 Corinthians 15:42, 43). This dimension of salvation awaits the coming day of eternity.

I affirm that the atonement, Jesus' death on the cross, purchased not only our soul's salvation but our total salvation, including that of our bodies. But the Scripture also affirms that we are "waiting for our adoption, to wit, the redemption of our body," and "we with patience wait for it" (Romans 8:23-25).

Many times the church gathers to pray, and in answer people are blessed with healing. We serve a God who can and does restore many to health in response to our intercession. Yet we still face a mortal's death. We face sickness and suffering on occasion. When God chooses to restore us to health, we are grateful. When the pains remain, we will not question either God's goodness or our faith. We know full health was purchased in the atonement and will be ours at the adoption, if we are among the acquitted.

Healing Is for the Acquitted

Healing was purchased in the past at the atonement. Healing will be enjoyed at "the adoption" in the future. Healing is an experience for those acquitted in the present.

The Bible chapter we are concentrating on in this study of healing is in the book of Romans. The theme of that book is justification by faith in Christ. To be justified is to be vindicated. It is to be acquitted of charges. Romans 8 holds out its promise of hope and healing to the ones acquitted.

We find Paul arguing in the first three chapters of Romans that all men are lost in sin. Chapter 1 claims that all Gentiles are lost. Chapter 2 asserts that all Jews are lost. And chapter 3 avers that everybody is lost.

But then starts the good news. Chapter 4 heralds that all people can be saved by faith. Chapter 5 firmly declares that they can be saved from death. Chapter 6 says they can be saved from sin. Chapter 7 asserts that they can be saved from the law. Chapter 8 adds that they can be saved from condemnation. That is where we are—Romans 8.

In this segment of Romans, Paul confesses to groaning in the body while waiting for his adoption (Romans 8:23). Yet he knows that resurrection day will come for him, for he has been acquitted.

Where is this vindication found, so we can claim the promise of healing? Where is this justification obtained, so we can one day know wholeness? The book of Romans begins with the answer to that question as well: "The gospel . . . is the power of God unto salvation to every one that believeth" (Romans 1:16). Believers in Christ's gospel are acquitted. Scattered throughout the book the same answer echoes. Hear chapter 5: "Being therefore justified by faith, we have peace with God through our Lord Jesus Christ" (5:1). Hear chapter 6: "We were buried therefore with him through baptism into death: that like as Christ was raised from the dead through the glory of the Father, so we also might walk in newness of life" (6:4). Hear chapter 8: "There is therefore now no condemnation to them that are in Christ Jesus. For the law of the Spirit of life in Christ Jesus made me free from the law of sin and of death" (8:1, 2). Hear chapter 10: "If thou shalt confess with thy mouth Jesus as Lord, and shalt believe in thy heart that God raised him from the dead, thou shalt be saved: for with the heart man believeth unto righteousness; and with the mouth confession is made unto salvation" (10:9, 10).

All the way through Romans runs the assurance that you will have the blessing of the atonement at the final advent of Christ, if you have previously been acquitted. Paul makes it clear that Jesus' disciples will know suffering. They will not get by without having at least some of the difficulties that befall the rest of humanity. But he guarantees that, if they come under the blood of the cross their sins will be covered and they will rise one day to die no more. That body will have every sickness healed, every pain gone, and every tear wiped away. May we "with patience wait for it" (Romans 8:25).

>My heavenly home is bright and fair;
>Nor pain nor death can enter there.
>Its glittering towers the sun outshine;
>That heavenly mansion shall be mine.
>
>-William Hunter

6

Abundance

of pardon to enjoy
of people to embrace
of purpose to encounter
of pain to endure
of power to enable

6

The Promise of Abundance

When Old Testament prophets told of the coming new age, the Christian era, they sang of prosperity, plenty, and joy (Isaiah 60:1-5, 17; 61:1-6). Church hymns of today echo the same refrain.

> "All things are ready," come to the feast!
> Come, for the table now is spread;
> Ye famishing, ye weary, come,
> And thou shalt be richly fed.[1]

Speaking to those who had suffered much under unfaithful religious leaders, Jesus told them He had come to be the Good Shepherd. He said, "I came that they may have life, and may have it abundantly" (John 10:10). His miracles reflected the abundance He came to bring. In the only miracle recorded in all four of the Gospels, Jesus fed a multitude. It was a crowd of five thousand men, with uncounted women and children. He began with a young lad's lunch of but "five barley loaves, and two fishes." Yet after each person was filled, there remained twelve baskets full (John 6:13).

Bible miracles speak of abundance. Church hymns sing of abundance. Jesus' promises talk of abundance. The parable of the prodi-

---

[1] Charlotte G. Homer, "Come to the Feast," *Christian Hymns III* (Nashville: Gospel Advocate Co., 1956), p. 12. Used by permission.

gal son is one of the best known of Jesus' stories. You recall that the prodigal, when far away from his father's house, became famished with hunger. He recalled that at home even servants had "bread enough and to spare." He was right. Upon his return to the father's house, "the fatted calf" provided an abundant meal of glad celebration (Luke 15:11-32).

It is of tremendous importance that we properly understand the promise of abundant life. I fear that some mistakenly expect an abundance of earthly possessions because Jesus promised life abundant. A few radio preachers and TV evangelists seem to give their hearers the impression that financial blessings and physical health will come in abundance, if they but have proper faith and give sacrificially.

We would be well advised to check our human interpretation of this promise of abundance by divine understanding. Compare what Jesus pledged in John 10:10 with His teaching in Luke 12:15. There He taught, "Take heed, and keep yourselves from all covetousness: for a man's life consisteth not in the abundance of the things which he possesseth."

That makes sense. If Jesus lived in our day, likely He would not sleep in sheets of satin or drive expensive limousines. He at times had "not where to lay his head" (Matthew 8:20). His early followers in many places gave up everything, including their lives, for their Messiah. Paul wrote when a prisoner, "I know how to be abased, and I know also how to abound: in everything and in all things have I learned the secret both to be filled and to be hungry, both to abound and to be in want. I can do all things in him that strengtheneth me" (Philippians 4:12, 13).

According to the Sermon on the Mount, they that hunger and thirst after righteousness shall be filled (Matthew 5:6). This promise of abundance is not a promise that we will have an abundance of things. It is a promise of an abundance of righteousness and all that overflows therefrom.

An Abundance of Pardon to Enjoy

Let the wicked forsake his way, and the unrighteous man his thoughts; and let him return unto Jehovah, and he will have mercy upon him; and to our God, for he will abundantly pardon.

—Isaiah 55:7

Life does not consist in the abundance of worldly possessions. But "blessed is he whose transgression is forgiven, whose sin is covered" (Psalm 32:1). As Paul declared, "where sin abounded, grace did abound more exceedingly" (Romans 5:20). The Christian life knows the joyful fulness of an abundant pardon.

Follow that woman as she walks off the street and enters the house of Simon the Pharisee. Notice what she does, to the embarrassment of the host. She stands at Jesus' feet and begins to weep uncontrollable tears. She lets her hair down to wipe those tears off Jesus' feet.

In total disgust Simon questions how Jesus can be considered a prophet when He apparently does not even know what kind of a woman is touching Him.

Jesus asks permission to tell Simon a story about a lender who had two debtors. One owed five hundred shillings and the other owed fifty. Since the lender forgave both debts, Jesus asks which of the debtors will appreciate the lender the more. That question He poses to His critical host. The Pharisee answers, "He, I suppose, to whom he forgave the most." By this simple parable, Jesus makes it clear that those abundantly pardoned by God will love Him abundantly (Luke 7:36-50).

See that man push ahead of the Jericho crowd and climb the sycamore for a view of Jesus. His name is Zacchaeus. He is a hated tax collector, yet Jesus asks to stay with him and says, "Today is salvation come to this house" (Luke 19:1-9). When even open sinners and detested tax collectors for pagan powers can be forgiven, that is abundant pardon.

Ascend Calvary with the crowd and see the malefactor being crucified with Jesus. There is no question about his recent offense. But listen to Jesus' gracious words upon the thief's plea, "Jesus, remember me": "To-day shalt thou be with me in Paradise" (Luke 23:39-43). That is abundant pardon.

Walk behind Saul of Tarsus on his way toward Damascus. There he intends to search out the men and women who have become followers of the way. These he plans to drag into prison, and he will raise his voice against them, seeking that they may die for their faith. But Jesus appears to him on the road, and later sends Ananias to inform him that he can be baptized and wash away his sins (Acts 22:3-16). That is abundant pardon.

If you have sinned, do not despair. The Scripture promises that God will cast your sins into the depth of the sea (Micah 7:19). He will remember them no more (Jeremiah 31:34). He will remove them as far as the east is from the west (Psalm 103:12). Your abundance as a Christian will include the abundant pardon of God.

God's promised abundance for you is not a promise of material good. Many people satiated in worldly possessions do not know God's joy. But multitudes in humble surroundings confess to the inner peace of forgiveness that goes with abundant living through Christ.

An Abundant People to Embrace

How can people speak with straight faces about living the abundant life when some of them are unemployed and unsure where the money will come from to meet tomorrow's expenses? What do they mean? More important, what did Jesus mean when He promised them an abundant life? The answer is found in His teaching. He promised an abundant pardon for us to enjoy. He promised an abundance of people for us to embrace.

What a joy it is to stand outside the place of worship before each service, and one by one greet the family of God! Some in that family know what the Lord meant when He spoke of having to leave "houses, or brethren, or sisters, or father, or mother, or children, or lands" for His sake. They also have learned the truth of His promise that they "shall receive a hundredfold, and shall inherit eternal life" (Matthew 19:29).

When told that His mother and brothers were looking for Him, Jesus "stretched forth his hand towards his disciples, and said, Behold, my mother and my brethren! For whosoever shall do the will of my Father who is in heaven, he is my brother, and sister, and mother" (Matthew 12:46-50). "So then ye are no more strangers and sojourners, but ye are fellow-citizens with the saints, and of the household of God" (Ephesians 2:19).

"I'm so glad I'm a part of the family of God," goes the familiar song. "I'm so glad I'm a part of the family of God," goes each beat of my heart. At local church assemblies, at state and national conventions, I thrill with the size of God's growing family. Visiting mission stations around the world, one sleeps in a hut at a fishing village in Africa or eats a simple meal seated on the floor with newfound friends in India. He finds that just because he wears the name Christian he is accepted. Jesus' followers, although they do not talk his language, immediately open the doors of hearts and homes to him. They count him a brother in the Lord. It is no less than Jesus who makes you "abound in love one toward another" (1 Thessalonians 3:12). They are no less than His ambassadors who "exhort you . . . that ye abound more and more" (1 Thessalonians 4:10) in that loving acceptance.

Christian friends constitute a great portion of the abundance that the believer possesses. There is an abundance of persons that you can "throw your arms around." Never again will you be alone and without family. The Heavenly Father has many children, and they all are brothers and sisters to the born-again.

An Abundant Purpose to Encounter

As we trace the words *abundant* and *abundance* throughout the Christian Scriptures, do those Bible passages promise material possessions and an abundance of things? They rather deny these. Instead I find promise of an abundant pardon and an abundance of real friends who will not let me down. Scriptures further inform me that I will have an abundant purpose. I will have something to do of eternal significance in my world. As God's instrument, I have something to live for—a reason for being.

Whether the Christian is twenty-one or one hundred and one, that person has a significant task to do on earth. Paul in his fifties claimed to have "labored more abundantly than they all" (1 Corinthians 15:10). He admonished the rest: "Wherefore, my beloved brethren, be ye stedfast, unmovable, always abounding in the work of the Lord, forasmuch as ye know that your labor is not vain in the Lord" (1 Corinthians 15:58). How could each Christian give so much of himself? Paul replied, "God is able to make all grace abound unto you; that ye, having always all sufficiency in everything, may abound unto every good work" (2 Corinthians 9:8).

The apostle could see the world through the eyes of Jesus. The work was abundant and the laborers few (Matthew 9:36-38). The "whole creation" (Mark 16:15) was to be reached with the gospel of saving grace. Paul found purpose in fulfilling that still unfulfilled mission.

> O Zion, haste, thy mission high fulfilling,
>   To tell to all the world that God is Light;
>   That He who made all nations is not willing
>   One soul should perish, lost in shades of night.
>   —Mary Ann Thomson

An Abundant Pain to Endure

We pray, "Lord, I want an abundant life." He answers, "It is not found in things; it is found in God's great forgiveness, His great family of people, and His great commission that gives your life purpose."

It might be good if we could stop here. But the Bible describes the Christian's life by adding another abundance. We need to be attentive to what else is said, lest we misread Christ's promise. Searching the Scriptures, we find an abundance of pain is foretold.

Have you heard people call attention to Revelation 7:14 and what it says about "the great tribulation"? Let me translate that phrase differently. Let me word it "the abundance of troubles." John writes in his apocalypse about these trials, aware that God's Old Testament prophets had been martyred and the New Testament apostles, friends of John, had died already for their faith. Near the beginning of his book of Revelation, he addresses the readers, saying, "I John, your brother and partaker with you in the tribulation" (Revelation 1:9).

Paul, as early as his first missionary journey, informed new believers "that through many tribulations [i.e., abundant troubles] we must enter into the kingdom of God" (Acts 14:22).

Is that the way it is? That is the way it was for the earliest Jerusalem Christians. They were dispersed by persecution. One of their great leaders wrote, "Count it all joy, my brethren, when ye fall into manifold temptations [abundant trials]; knowing that the proving of your faith worketh patience" (James 1:2, 3).

> Must Jesus bear the cross alone,
> And all the world go free?
> No; there's a cross for every one,
> And there's a cross for me.
> —Thomas Shepherd

At one time the sons of Zebedee may have seen themselves sitting on thrones at either side of Christ (Mark 10:35-37). But James died as the first apostolic martyr (Acts 12:1, 2); and John recorded Jesus' words, "In the world ye have tribulation: but be of good cheer; I have overcome the world" (John 16:33).

Jesus wanted none to follow Him that did not know the cost. As early as the giving of the Beatitudes, He was teaching,

Blessed are they that have been persecuted for righteousness' sake: for theirs is the kingdom of heaven. Blessed are ye when men shall reproach you, and persecute you, and say all manner of evil against you falsely, for my sake. Rejoice, and be exceeding glad: for great is your reward in heaven.
—Matthew 5:10-12

Paul understood that the Master had revealed a cup to drink, and it would be bitter. There was a baptism to undergo, and it would be an immersion of suffering (Mark 10:38, 39). Paul explained why he had given up his honored place among the Jews: "That I may know him, and the power of his resurrection, and the fellowship of his sufferings" (Philippians 3:10). He pleaded with Timothy, "Suffer hardship with me, as a good soldier of Christ Jesus" (2 Timothy 2:3). He informed the Romans that as followers of Christ "we also rejoice in our tribulations: knowing that tribulation worketh stedfastness" (Romans 5:3).

What gave the apostle to the Gentiles such a willingness to walk such a hard road? He informs us that "we are children of God: and if children, then heirs; heirs of God, and joint-heirs with Christ; if so be that we suffer with him" (Romans 8:16, 17).

Peter refers to our suffering just because we wear the name *Christian* (1 Peter 4:16). Luke tells of the advance of the army of God from the city of Jerusalem to the capital city of Rome. He tells of victories, but he tells of battles fought to win those victories. The soldiers of the cross knew "the abundant life," but they also knew abundant battle scars.

An Abundant Power to Enable

Should you read the story of valiant heroes of the faith winning new territory for Christ through struggle, torture, and death, you will seek the source of their strength. They smile through adversity. They conquer their enemies by sheer love. They have an abundant power within that enables selfless living.

Earlier I made reference to the Philippian passage where Paul tells how he "learned the secret both . . . to abound and to be in want." The secret was "I can do all things in him that strengtheneth me" (Philippians 4:12, 13).

No Scripture has been more misused than Philippians 4:13. It is often taken out of context and handed to novice believers, implying that they can literally do anything through Christ's aid. They can jump over the moon, raise the dead, walk on water, and turn water into wine. But read the context, verses 11-13. What Paul is teaching is that when prosperity comes your way, it need not spoil you. If trouble comes your way, you can handle it. Thank God for the enabling power of Jesus in any and all circumstances. You can meet all difficulties through Christ.

One living the abundant life in Christ can say with Isaiah, "They that wait for Jehovah shall renew their strength; they shall mount up with wings as eagles; they shall run, and not be weary; they shall walk, and not faint" (Isaiah 40:31).

You can handle life "under the circumstances," whatever they may be. You can do this because, in Christ who strengtheneth you, you live "above" those circumstances. You are in the care of Him "that is able to do exceeding abundantly above all that we ask or think, according to the power that worketh in us" (Ephesians 3:20).

The eyewitnesses of Jesus' resurrection were given the seemingly impossible assignment of evangelizing the world. Jesus said, "Ye shall be my witnesses both in Jerusalem, and in all Judaea and Samaria, and unto the uttermost part of the earth." But He also promised, "Ye shall receive power, when the Holy Spirit is come upon you" (Acts 1:8). When Christ gives an assignment to anyone, He clothes that one "with power from on high" (Luke 24:49) to fulfill the task given.

What kind of power is available to me and to you today? Whatever power we need to carry out God's will for our lives. Do not worry about lacking the power to bring new revelation and confirm it by miracles. The apostles had that power, for their age needed to receive the new gospel and see it confirmed (Mark 16:20). We are assigned the task of sharing the gospel with others, and Christ will enable us to succeed in that.

Many in Bible times were demon-possessed. In our times we need more who are divinely-possessed: controlled by God's Spirit. Those possessed by Satan go out to get, get, get and get some more. Those possessed by the Savior go out to give themselves, give themselves, give themselves to share the abundant life with others.

In the words of Lloyd Douglas, such selfless living is the "Magnificent Obsession." To live with purpose, to live with people, to live with passion for others, to live with pain for the lost world, and to live with power to see the mission of pardon through to the end—that is abundant living.

7

Promise of the Spirit

His Presence
  lest I be lonely

His Power
  lest I be weak

His Purging
  lest I be lost

His Purpose
  lest I be aimless

7

The Promise of the Holy Spirit

"Every promise in the Book is mine." So says a favorite chorus. Actually that is a hyperbole, an exaggeration for the sake of emphasis. Every chapter of the Bible has meaning for me, and every promise may affect me directly or indirectly; but not all of the promises are mine. If I trust the Lord and give my life to Him, then every promise that God meant for me is mine. But the Bible has many promises that were not meant for me.

For instance, when I read Genesis 12:1-3 I know with certainty that this promise is not for me, but was for Abraham: "Get thee out of thy country, and from thy kindred, and from thy father's house, unto the land that I will show thee: and I will make of thee a great nation."

Joshua was promised that the walls of Jericho would fall down when he and his army had marched around them according to instructions, and had climaxed their march with the blowing of trumpets and the shout of the people (Joshua 6:1-5). In no way is that promise to be claimed by any modern reader of the ancient story. That was a Bible promise, but the promise was not meant for any twentieth-century man.

The vital question before us regards God's promised gift of His Holy Spirit. Is that promise to me? Is that promise to you? Or is the promised Spirit of God only for the apostles?

With Bibles open to Acts, chapters 1 and 2, let us read the words carefully. We note first of all that the title men have given to Luke's writing is "The Acts of the *Apostles*." As we read, I want you to notice the nouns and pronouns printed in italics. Note the nouns I have inserted in brackets by some pronouns.

> The former treatise I made, O Theophilus, concerning all that Jesus began both to do and to teach, until the day in which he was received up, after that he had given commandment through the Holy Spirit unto the *apostles* whom he had chosen: to *whom* [the apostles] he also showed himself alive after his passion by many proofs, appearing unto *them* [the apostles] by the space of forty days, and speaking the things concerning the kingdom of God: and, being assembled together with *them* [the apostles], he charged *them* [the apostles] not to depart from Jerusalem, but to wait for the promise of the Father, which, said he, *ye* [the apostles] heard from me: for John indeed baptized with water; but ye [the apostles] shall be baptized in the Holy Spirit not many days hence.
> —Acts 1:1-8

To conserve time, let us bypass some of the chapter and go to the latter verses of Acts, chapter 1. Peter speaks to about 120 disciples gathered together. He talks about Judas' falling away and the need to find one to replace him as "a witness . . . of his [Christ's] resurrection" (verse 22).

The disciples look over their number and find two who are qualified. Not wanting to make the choice themselves, they call out in prayer to the Lord, "Thou, Lord, who knowest the hearts of all men, show of these two the one whom thou hast chosen, to take the place in this ministry and apostleship from which Judas fell away" (verses 24, 25). Lots are cast with the expectation that the Lord will determine the result.

> And the lot fell upon Matthias; and he was numbered with the eleven *apostles*. And when the day of Pentecost was now come, *they* [the apostles] were all together in one place. And suddenly there came from heaven a sound as of the rushing of a mighty wind, and it filled all the house where *they* [the apostles] were sitting. And there appeared unto *them* [the apostles] tongues parting asunder, like as of fire; and it sat

upon each one of *them* [the apostles]. And *they* [the apostles] were all filled with the Holy Spirit, and began to speak with other tongues, as the Spirit gave *them* [the apostles] utterance.
—Acts 1:26—2:4

We are entering a discussion on the promise of the Holy Spirit's indwelling. What we have read thus far in Acts has promised that Spirit to the apostles alone.

If not "every promise in the Book is mine," is the promise regarding the Spirit mine? Is it yours? Or is it only for Christ's apostles?

I have good news! Keep reading on into the second chapter of Acts. The inspired apostles are on their feet, and Peter begins to quote from the prophet Joel:

And it shall be in the last days, saith God, I will pour forth of my Spirit upon all flesh: and your sons and your daughters shall prophesy, and your young men shall see visions, and your old men shall dream dreams: yea and on my servants and on my handmaidens in those days will I pour forth of my Spirit; and they shall prophesy.
—Acts 2:17, 18

The great promise beginning to be fulfilled on that day speaks of God's Spirit coming upon young and old (no age discrimination), all flesh (no racial discrimination), servants and handmaidens (no sex discrimination). The promise of the Spirit certainly was not limited to the apostles. God's Spirit was to be poured out on others also, and He would give some of those others the gift of prophecy.

After these lengthy but necessary preliminary remarks, we are ready to zero in on the marvelous promise that climaxed the sermon of Pentecost:

Repent ye, and be baptized every one of you in the name of Jesus Christ unto the remission of your sins; and ye shall receive the gift of the Holy Spirit. For to you is the promise, and to your children, and to all that are afar off, even as many as the Lord our God shall call unto him.
—Acts 2:38, 39

What can we now conclude? First, it is evident that Christ's apostles received a very special measure of the Holy Spirit to equip them for their unique ministry as witnesses to Jesus' resurrection (Acts 2:1-4). Second, the Spirit gave the power of prophecy to others besides the apostles—to people of all kinds, but not to every person. The prophets were few enough to be remarkable (Acts 11:27, 28; 21:9). Third, the good news is that all who belong to Jesus Christ are indwelt by His Spirit. Not only *can* men be indwelt by God's Spirit, they *must* be if they are to be numbered among the children of God (Romans 8:9).

"Every promise in the Book is mine?" No. But this one is mine. With J. Oatman Jr. I can sing,

> I am so happy in Christ today
> That I go singing along my way;
> Yes, I'm so happy to know and say,
> Jesus included me too.

We Need His Presence

How grateful we are to be included! We need His presence lest we be lonely. As we sometimes sing:

> I've seen the lightning flashing;
>   I've heard the thunder roll,
> I've felt sin's breakers dashing,
>   Which almost conquered my soul;
> I've heard the voice of my Savior,
>   Bidding me still to fight on,
> He promised never to leave me,
>   Never to leave me alone.

Christ is with us as He promised: "Lo, I am with you always, even unto the end of the world" (Matthew 28:19, 20). That promise was spoken to the apostles, yes; but as we accept their task of making disciples, we claim the accompanying promise. Jesus is with us through His Spirit.

In Seattle, Washington, is an Indian Mission operated by one of my Timothys, Donald Summers. He sends out a monthly periodical called "Smoke Signals." I am grateful that in one of the issues Don, or a secretary, or a printer made a delightful mistake. An article spoke of "the indwelling *presents* of the Holy Spirit," where "the indwelling *presence* of the Holy Spirit" was meant.

We do enjoy many presents from God's Spirit. Some of His gifts are mentioned in the twelfth chapter of 1 Corinthians. We rejoice in such presents, but most of all we appreciate His presence within us. This is the gift we glory in just now. The Holy Spirit is given to us when we are baptized into Christ (Acts 2:38), and after that He lives in each one of us (1 Corinthians 6:19). None of us need walk alone. A Christian is never in a lonely apartment all by himself. He is not alone as he walks down a dark, deserted street. Christ is in him through the Spirit, and so he is never totally by himself.

The Holy Spirit is often called the "Spirit of God" or "the Spirit of Christ." Before Jesus left His disciples, He promised them "another Comforter," the Spirit of truth, the Holy Spirit (John 14:16, 17, 26). And He added "I come unto you" (John 14:18). In further explanation He said, "If a man love me, he will keep my word: and my Father will love him, and we will come unto him, and make our abode with him" (John 14:23). When the Holy Spirit is with us, both Jesus and the Father are with us.

No Christian needs to be alone. God wants to live in every heart. Paul was right when he wrote, "Christ in you, the hope of glory" (Colossians 1:27). On another occasion he affirmed,

> I have been crucified with Christ; and it is no longer I that live, but Christ liveth in me: and that life which I now live in the flesh I live in faith, the faith which is in the Son of God, who loved me, and gave himself up for me.
> —Galatians 2:20

This divine presence within is not just a temporary gift. Jesus assured the disciples in these words: "I will pray the Father, and he shall give you another Comforter, that he may be with you for ever" (John 14:16). Likewise "for ever" is the abiding presence with each Christian (1 Corinthians 6:19). Jesus does not want your life to be empty. He wants to fill you with His very presence to enrich your life with His comfort and help.

We Need His Power

Have you claimed the promise of Acts 2:38? Upon repentance and baptism, the believer is assured of both the Spirit's presence and His power. We need His presence lest we be lonely. We must have His power lest we be weak.

I do not want to live a lonely life, so I want His presence with me. I do not want to live a feeble life, so I desire His power within. I ask myself day by day, "Can I live the Christian life? Can I do all my Lord wants me to do?" And the answer is, "Not in your own strength, but Christ's power is available."

According to Acts 1:8, Jesus informed His official witnesses, the apostles, that they were to cover the city of Jerusalem, the nation of Israel, and the entire world with His message. The strength by which they would carry out such a daring assignment would be the power of His Holy Spirit.

Are you living with God's enabling power? Often I use an overhead projector in preaching and teaching. It may for many days be sitting in a storeroom cold and dark. Then on another day it is in use. The glass is the same, the light bulb is the same, the housing is the same, the cord is the same; but something is different when the machine is in use. It has been plugged into the socket, into the power.

When I was a boy of high-school age, one of my daily tasks was to saw enough wood for the furnace, the cook stove, and the fireplace. Unfortunately, I did not know about power saws. With no power but my own, it took a great deal of muscle and sweat to do the job. With a power saw much more could have been done in less time and with less distress on my part.

A wonderful fact of Christian living is that you not only enjoy the holy presence of the Spirit, but also thrill with the holy power of the Spirit. That does not mean you can do every fanciful thing you would like to do, but it does mean you can do whatever difficult thing God wants you to do.

Doesn't Philippians 4:13 mean a great deal? It reads, "I can do all things in him that strengtheneth me." Paul thankfully prayed, "I thank him that enabled me" (1 Timothy 1:12) and he happily observed that "God gave us not a spirit of fearfulness; but of power" (2 Timothy 1:7). The apostles were not to start their great work till they were "clothed with power from on high" (Luke 24:49). If you feel weak, just remember the song of your childhood:

> Jesus loves me! this I know,
> For the Bible tells me so;
> Little ones to Him belong;
> They are weak, but He is strong.
> —Anna B. Warner

Or hear some male quartet harmonize in "Just a Closer Walk With Thee." When they begin the first stanza of the song, open your ears wide:

> I am weak, but Thou art strong;
> Jesus, keep me from all wrong.

We Need His Purging

The Heavenly Father's promise is for everyone. If you will receive Him, His presence will be there lest you be lonely. His power will be there lest you be weak. And His purging will be there lest you be lost.

The Spirit of God works through the Word of God to purge out of a life evil habits and wicked thoughts. The Spirit inspired the Bible so that it is truly God's Word. In Ephesians 6:17 "the word of God" is said to be "the sword of the Spirit," the implement or tool He uses to accomplish His purpose. So it was in the days of the psalmist. He asked, "Wherewith shall a young man cleanse his way?" He answered, "By taking heed thereto according to thy word" (Psalm 119:9). Paul in New Testament times speaks his agreement:

> I beseech you therefore, brethren, by the mercies of God, to present your bodies a living sacrifice, holy, acceptable to God, which is your spiritual service. And be not fashioned according to this world: but be ye transformed by the renewing of your mind.
> —Romans 12:1, 2

Through the inspired Word the Spirit renews the mind, turning it away from evil thoughts and evil desires. Meanwhile the Spirit living within the person gives him power to live by the prompting of his renewed mind. With the power of the Spirit you can do what you know is right. Temptation is still with you, yes; but none that you cannot overcome (1 Corinthians 10:13).

This is the way one is transformed, cleansed, and purged. The Holy Spirit works through the Word. The Word reveals Jesus in all His perfection. The more you look at Jesus in the Word, the more the Holy Spirit transforms you into Christ's image.

Justification and sanctification are important Bible ideas. Paul wrote to the Corinthians about them. Listen to what he said:

Know ye not that the unrighteous shall not inherit the kingdom of God? Be not deceived: neither fornicators, nor idolaters, nor adulterers, nor effeminate, nor abusers of themselves with men, nor thieves, nor covetous, nor drunkards, nor revilers, nor extortioners, shall inherit the kingdom of God. And such were some of you: but ye were washed, but ye were sanctified, but ye were justified in the name of the Lord Jesus Christ, and in the Spirit of our God.

—1 Corinthians 6:9-11

One is cleansed and sanctified and justified when he becomes a Christian and the Holy Spirit comes to live within him.

When Jesus went around exorcizing demons, He told a story to illustrate that casting out a demon was not enough. He told of putting an evil spirit out of a man and giving the man a thorough housecleaning to make him ready for the next occupant. To cast a demon out of a life without bringing in a new occupant would not do. A life unoccupied by the Holy Spirit would invite the exiled demon to come back, bringing more evil spirits with him (Matthew 12:43-45).

Our lives do need cleansing. They also need the Holy Spirit to live in them and keep them holy. Peter told his hearers that upon their baptism two things would happen: something would be taken away and something would be added. Their sins would be removed, and their lives would be filled with the Spirit (Acts 2:38). In other words, when the house is cleansed, the Holy Spirit becomes the new resident or occupant to keep it that way.

We Need His Purpose

Purpose is important to the enjoyment of life. As surely as we need God's presence and power and purging, we need His purpose. Without purpose, life is as aimless as a boat without a rudder.

Recently I heard a professor from Pacific Christian College tell his students the meaning of the word *mediocre*. *Ocris* is a Latin word for a mountain. *Medius* is the middle or halfway point. Hence a mediocre person is one who goes only halfway up the mountain. Such an individual does not scale to the top, but settles for less. The challenge of the professor's message was this: If we want to go all the way with Christ, we must have a purpose and intend from the start to reach this set goal.

The rifleman has to have a target. The football team must know where the goal is. The pilot taking off at the international airport needs to head for a definite destination.

Every man needs something to live *on*. He needs a standard to live *by*. And he also must have a purpose to live *for*.

When the Spirit of God fills a life with His presence, His power, and His purging, He gives also a reason for living. Some elderly persons stagnate after retirement, for they have lost their purpose. I tell you that every person who lives for Jesus Christ has a reason to press on, be he young or old. In the church there is meaning and purpose and reason for being. There is Christ's mission to fulfill, and every life is needed.

Jesus had a purpose and He made it known: "The Son of man also came not to be ministered unto, but to minister, and to give his life a ransom for many" (Mark 10:45). He "came to seek and to save that which was lost" (Luke 19:10). He had a goal and He reached His goal.

What about the apostles? They could not ransom others with their lives, but they were to carry on their Master's mission of seeking and saving, and in this the Holy Spirit was to be their helper. Just before Jesus ascended back to Heaven He told His apostles, "When the Holy Spirit is come upon you . . . ye shall be my witnesses" (Acts 1:8).

Acts 8:29 records that Philip was guided by the Spirit to share the gospel with a man of Ethiopia. That is to say, the Holy Spirit led him to serve the same purpose Jesus had, which was to win the lost.

In Acts 13:1, 2 we read about missionaries. "The Holy Spirit said, Separate me Barnabas and Saul for the work whereunto I have called them." In the body of Christ, filled by the Spirit of Christ, are the people of Christ carrying out the purpose of Christ to save mankind. The final chapter of the Bible again joins the Holy Spirit to the church in its mission of evangelism: "The Spirit and the bride say, Come" (Revelation 22:17).

What conclusion are we to draw? The purpose of Jesus is plain. Is it your purpose? Will you give yourself in the service of others, that all people may be won to the Lord?

Look at the promise of the Holy Spirit one more time. It is found most clearly in Acts 2:38, 39. It tells every reader who it is to whom God is ready to give His Spirit.

Believers are told to repent. I must define that to avoid any misunderstanding. The English word *repent* is the translation of the Greek verb *metanoeo*. Basically it means to change one's mind. Dwight L. Moody told his audiences that repentance did not have to do with their handkerchiefs but with their wills. To cry crocodile tears is no substitute for what God asks in repentance, but sincere grief may lead one to repent. "Godly sorrow worketh repentance" (2 Corinthians 7:10). Repentance demands an act of will, a making up of the mind to turn from sin to the Lord.

Sunday after Sunday after Sunday, sermons are preached and invitations are extended to the lost to accept Jesus as their personal Savior. Many remain in their pews, not because they do not believe the gospel, but because they will not make the life-changing decision. They will not make up their minds and commit their lives to the service of Jesus.

"Repent and be baptized," said Peter. When one has made up his mind to obey Jesus, his burial in water dramatizes the end of the old way when life was lived for self. His rising from the watery grave announces the beginning of a different life—a life indwelt by Christ's Spirit and spent in the service of others.

The promise of Acts 2:38, the promise of the Spirit's indwelling, was not just to the three thousand converts on Pentecost. "For to you is the promise, and to your children, and to all that are afar off, even as many as the Lord our God shall call unto him" (verse 39).

The offer of God is made to all, but not all receive it. Be one who says yes to Heaven's offer.

8

Jesus, Keep Me

by the warranty

from the wrong

in the way

under the Word

at the work

8

The Promise of Security

> He saves, He keeps, He satisfies,
>   This wonderful friend of mine.
> Some day I'll meet Him in the skies,
>   This wonderful friend divine.[1]

That chorus is true. Jesus saves, Jesus keeps those whom He saves. And Jesus fills each saved life with satisfaction. While Jesus promises all three of these blessed experiences, we want now to consider just His promise to keep His own.

Throughout the Scripture is found the verb *keep* and also the noun *keeper*. We want to limit our present investigation to this word *keep*, and further restrict our study to those times this word is used as a promise.

Our interest is not now in the command *keep*. "Jehovah is in his holy temple: let all the earth keep silence before him" (Habakkuk 2:20). This is a command. Paul pleaded, "Keep the unity of the Spirit in the bond of peace" (Ephesians 4:3). Solomon's imperative was, "Fear God, and keep his commandments" (Ecclesiastes 12:13). These are commands from God to be obeyed, not promises from God for us to enjoy. The Old Covenant admonitions to keep the

---
[1] Copyrighted by Ray Osterhouse, address unknown.

Passover and keep the Sabbath and keep the Covenant likewise are commands. Just now we investigate not what regulations we are ordered to keep, but God's promise to keep us.

Other times in the Bible the word *keep* or *kept* is used in the simple statement of a fact. Luke, for instance, tells how Mary, Jesus' mother, "kept all these sayings in her heart" (Luke 2:51). Still other times in the Scripture *keep* or *kept* is part of a warning, as when Peter speaks of the heavens and earth "being reserved [or kept] against the day of judgment and destruction of ungodly men" (2 Peter 3:7).

"Jehovah bless thee, and keep thee . . . lift up his countenance upon thee, and give thee peace," reads Numbers 6:24, 26. The word *keep* is to be found in this passage, but it is here part of a benediction or a prayer rather than a promise. Therefore we bypass this text as well.

The promise of Christ to keep you and me is the object of our search at this time. It is the promise of security—the promise of His keeping our lives from here to eternity.

Jesus Keeps Us by the Warranty

Did you learn to pray at bedtime, "Now I lay me down to sleep, I pray the Lord my soul to keep"? Did you ever sing "Jesus, keep me lest I stray"?

We have the right so to pray and to sing, for we have that keeping promised, assured by divine warranty. Jude's epistle is addressed "to them that are called . . . and kept for Jesus Christ" (Jude 1). Think on that. We have been called. We are the church—the called out. Jesus uttered the invitation to come unto Him, and we have responded to the call. We now enjoy the fact that, as the called of Christ, we are being kept by Christ.

Just because some groups carry *their* doctrine of eternal security to an extreme, we should not avoid the *Biblical* doctrine regarding that glorious security. There is a Scriptural teaching of eternal security that ought not to be forfeited for some lesser doctrine of infernal insecurity. It was never God's intention that His children live in constant confusion as to whether they really are in His family. Jesus said,

> My sheep hear my voice, and I know them, and they follow me: and I give unto them eternal life; and they shall never

perish, and no one shall snatch them out of my hand. My Father, who hath given them unto me, is greater than all; and no one is able to snatch them out of the Father's hand.
—John 10:27-29

Those who are hearing Christ's voice and following Him are secure. Neither a man on earth nor a demon in Hell can take away this security that is found under the Shepherd's care.

Reveling in that certain security, Paul broke into a doxology to God. He asked, "Who shall separate us from the love of Christ?" He answered His own question:

> I am persuaded that neither death, nor life, nor angels, nor principalities, nor things present, nor things to come, nor powers, nor height, nor depth, nor any other creature, shall be able to separate us from the love of God, which is in Christ Jesus our Lord.
> —Romans 8:35, 38, 39

What a warranty! Christ will not break His promise. No outside force can annul the agreement He made with His own. Only the individual himself, the one who has accepted the Savior, can break that covenant with the Lord.

We have "an inheritance incorruptible, and undefiled, and that fadeth not away, reserved in heaven" (1 Peter 1:4). Christians are to walk in confidence. They are to have "the peace of God, which passeth all understanding" (Philippians 4:7). They are not to be ill at ease regarding their salvation. If they are hearing the Shepherd's voice and following His leading, they can affirm with Paul, "I know him whom I have believed, and I am persuaded that he is able to guard that which I have committed unto him against that day" (2 Timothy 1:12).

"Be thou faithful unto death" and "the crown of life" will be yours (Revelation 2:10). So said the resurrected Christ to His church. If you are abiding in the faith, you too have Heaven's warranty. Today, if you are in covenant with Christ, cast aside your fears, for "your life is hid with Christ in God" (Colossians 3:3). *With Christ* means you are safe. *In God* means you are doubly safe. If you have heard of Christ, believed in Christ, repented toward Christ, been baptized into Christ, and are being faithful to Christ, you are secure. You have God's word on that.

In Old Testament times there were cities of refuge (Numbers 35:9-28). Under certain circumstances a killer was safe inside their walls. No avenger could touch him unless he would leave the place of that security. In this New Testament era, we sinners can flee to Christ. He is our refuge. In Him we are secure. Only if we leave Him, turn our backs on Him, trample Him under foot, are we exposed to vengeance (see Hebrews 10:29).

When we buy a new refrigerator or a new car, we get a warranty. That warranty may have in it some small print we should have read. The warranty Christ gives to His church is in large print: "Be thou faithful unto death, and I will give thee the crown of life" (Revelation 2:10).

Jesus Keeps Us From the Wrong

When we pray, "Our Father who art in heaven, Hallowed be thy name," we petition, "bring us not into temptation, but deliver us from the evil one" (Matthew 6:9, 13). Jesus himself petitioned: "I pray not that thou shouldest take them from the world, but that thou shouldest keep them from the evil one" (John 17:15).

Here we learn that the Lord, who warrants that I will be kept safe if I remain in Christ, guarantees to make possible my escape from every wrong placed before me by the tempter. Hear the promise:

> There hath no temptation taken you but such as man can bear: but God is faithful, who will not suffer you to be tempted above that ye are able; but will with the temptation make also the way of escape, that ye may be able to endure it.
> —1 Corinthians 10:13

Hear also the assurance in the last lines of Jude's epistle: "Now unto him that is able to guard [or keep] you from stumbling" (Jude 24). Jude has just admonished the believers, "Keep yourselves in the love of God" (Jude 21). Now he assures them of God's ability to keep them from stumbling. Like Jude, a psalmist expressed appreciation for the Good Shepherd's care. He said, "For thou hast delivered my soul from death, mine eyes from tears, and my feet from falling" (Psalm 116:8). In another psalm we see the word *keep* several times: "I will lift up mine eyes unto the mountains: from whence shall my help come? My help cometh from Jehovah. . . . Jehovah is thy keeper. . . . Jehovah will keep thee from all evil; He will keep thy soul. Jehovah will keep thy going out and thy coming in from this time forth and for evermore" (121:1, 2, 5, 7, 8).

Being kept from falling under temptation is no small matter. The heart is deceived and the religion is vain if one does not "keep oneself unspotted from the world" (James 1:26, 27). The soul must sing sincerely, "I am weak but Thou art strong; Jesus, keep me from all wrong."

We need to remember that the promise to keep us is a promise that includes our being kept from wrong. But like every conditional promise, this one calls for cooperation from both parties of the agreement.

Jesus Keeps Us in the Way

Need I remind you that we need to rest in this promise of security? God will keep us by the warranty. He guarantees keeping us from the wrong by making a way of escape in all the temptations that come our way. Another way to put it is that He will keep you and me in the way. To be kept from evil is to be kept on the path of righteousness.

If we want to go to Heaven, there is no other way than the way of Christ. His is the name "wherein we must be saved" (Acts 4:12). Our plea, of necessity, is "Lord, keep me in that way—keep me in the body of Christ, the church. Keep me from dropping out or turning back."

From the early days of Christianity, Jesus' disciples were called followers "of the Way" (Acts 9:2). Jesus spoke of the Father's house and its many mansions. He said that He was going there and that they knew the way. When Thomas asked, "How know we the way?" Jesus said, "I am the way, and the truth, and the life: no one cometh unto the Father, but by me" (John 14:1-6).

Jesus' mission is to guide humans from earth to glory. All tempting detours are to be avoided. All competing voices crying out for us to follow them must be denied. Isaiah spoke of this one way to eternal life. He predicted, "And a highway shall be there, and a way, and it shall be called The way of holiness; the unclean shall not pass over it; but it shall be for the redeemed" (Isaiah 35:8).

The eloquent Apollos, mighty in the Scriptures, was seen by Priscilla and Aquila to be deficient in the gospel message. The only baptism he knew was the baptism of John. Luke records that this couple told the preacher more of the message they had heard from

Paul. Luke writes, "They took him unto them, and expounded unto him the way of God more accurately" (Acts 18:26).

"The way of God," "the way of holiness," "the way of life" is the way of Jesus. The broad way that many in this world travel is the way that leads to destruction, according to the Sermon on the Mount. But the Master Teacher also spoke of the narrow gate and the straitened way that lead to life (Matthew 7:13, 14). May we be among the few that find it.

Doesn't your heart rejoice when you see a soul "bid farewell to the way of the world to walk in it nevermore"? Do you not delight at some convert's baptism into Christ, picturing the burial of the old way and the rising to walk in a way totally new? (Romans 6:4). Yet do we not feel pain when, counting the sheep in the fold, we find that some have strayed away? We rightly are concerned, for we know that we were not promised *unconditional* security. We rather were promised *certain* security as long as we remained under the warranty, turned from the wrong, and lived in the way.

Jesus Keeps Us Under the Word

As a preacher of the gospel, I constantly pray that I will teach only the Word of Christ—the divine revelation—and that I will avoid the opinions of men as human detours. I seek to join those Christians who "speak where the Scriptures speak" and "are silent where the Scriptures are silent." I hope to avoid being influenced by those who feel the modern church should give up what they call the "narrow way." Jesus agrees that His way is narrow (Matthew 7:14), but faithfully following that narrow way is what we call sticking to the faith and practice of the apostolic church—"the faith which was once for all delivered unto the saints" (Jude 3).

The safe place to stand in preaching and teaching is near the cross and under the word of Him who died on the cross. Why do I say that? Because of what He said: "If ye abide in my word, then are ye truly my disciples" (John 8:31). Instead of seeking new theologies, Christ's disciples "abide" where the earliest followers stood.

Peter phrased it as a warning: "If any man speaketh" let him speak "as it were oracles of God" (1 Peter 4:11). That is to say, he who rises to preach is to preach the word God gave. He is not to present his human understanding as if it were equal in authority to divinely expressed truth. His audience has a right to receive a "thus saith the Lord" and not a "thus thinketh the preacher."

Paul charged a young evangelist to "preach the word," for that was Timothy's assigned task. He was to "preach the word; be urgent in season, out of season," for there would be times when it might seem unseasonable. Paul foretold what would be true in the life of Timothy and in the lives of all preachers since. He prophesied,

> The time will come when they will not endure the sound doctrine; but, having itching ears, will heap to themselves teachers after their own lusts; and will turn away their ears from the truth, and turn aside unto fables.
> —2 Timothy 4:3-4

Check out the fulfillment of that prophecy by looking at the churches advertised in next Saturday's paper or the churches listed in the yellow pages of the phone book. There is a religion for every whim and human liking. For whatever the ear itches to hear, a new faith will be invented.

In one of the last books of the New Testament to be written, John joins Peter and Paul in calling on the church to stay with the original gospel and not to adulterate or modify it. He pens, "Whosoever goeth onward and abideth not in the teaching of Christ, hath not God: he that abideth in the teaching, the same hath both the Father and the Son" (2 John 9).

Jesus warned His disciples of the ease wherewith "the precepts of men" and "the tradition of men," almost unnoticed, can replace "the commandment of God" (Mark 7:7, 8). While the Pharisees probably viewed their doctrines as only clarifying what the Scripture said, Jesus saw the end result and said they were "making void the word of God" by *their* "tradition" (Mark 7:13).

Let it not be man's word, but "the word of Christ" that you let "dwell in you richly" in your "teaching and admonishing one another" (Colossians 3:16). "Learn not to go beyond the things which are written" (1 Corinthians 4:6). Stay under the word as given by the Son of God.

Christ's word is the truth, the entire truth, and nothing but "the whole counsel of God" (Acts 20:27). "The word of God is living, and active, and sharper than any two-edged sword" (Hebrews 4:12). That Word is "inspired of God" and "profitable for teaching, for reproof, for correction, for instruction which is in righteousness: that the man of God may be complete, furnished completely unto every good work" (2 Timothy 3:16, 17). "I commend you to God, and to the word of his grace, which is able to build you up, and to give you the inheritance among all them that are sanctified" (Acts 20:32). Stick with the gospel. Stay by apostolic teaching. Remain under the word of Christ.

Jesus Keeps Us at the Work

It is good for us to pray that God will keep us securely all the way into the world eternal. And He will. Hearing and following the Good Shepherd's voice, we have that eternal salvation warranted. We also pray that the Lord will keep us from the wrong that would cause us to fall. We ask Him to keep us in the way, where we have His rod and staff to comfort us. As to what teaching we follow or ask others to follow, we ask that God will keep us under the Word as Christ gave it before men started changing it with additions here, deletions there, and alterations throughout.

Such prayers as we suggest above will not be too long, if we also pray that the Master keep us at the work. We may at times get tired *in* the work, but may Heaven keep us from ever tiring *of* the work.

Shall we complain that we have been teaching a Bible class for years and now it should be someone else's turn? Shall we lay down that share of the load we have been bearing in the church and ask another to take it up? May we not consider retirement from our spiritual jobs, as we do at a certain age from our secular occupations?

Before we answer, it behooves followers of Christ to listen to their Teacher. "My Father worketh even until now, and I work," Jesus said (John 5:17). To make Christ-likeness our aim means there is work to be done and service to be rendered by us. "The harvest indeed is plenteous, but the laborers are few" (Matthew 9:37). All hands are needed. And they are needed now, for "the night cometh, when no man can work" (John 9:4).

Partners in the growth of the kingdom are called by the apostles "fellow-workers" (Philippians 4:3). Women like Dorcas were honored for being "full of good works" (Acts 9:36). Preachers like Timothy were encouraged to "do the work of an evangelist" (2 Timothy 4:5). Potential elders were advised that "if a man seeketh the office of a bishop, he desireth a good work" (1 Timothy 3:1). Each teacher in the harness was ordered, "Give diligence to present thyself approved unto God, a workman that needeth not to be ashamed, handling aright the word of truth" (2 Timothy 2:15).

Let every Christian adjust his attitudes and ideas regarding work by what his God has recorded as His expressed will to man. Why has God redeemed us? "We are his workmanship, created in Christ Jesus for good works" (Ephesians 2:10). Christ "gave himself for us, that he might redeem us from all iniquity, and purify unto himself a people for his own possession, zealous of good works" (Titus 2:14).

When the dead are finally raised, they will be "judged every man according to their works" (Revelation 20:13). Those "who die in the Lord . . . rest from their labors" (Revelation 14:13). This suggests that until you die, you are to be "stedfast, unmovable, always abounding in the work of the Lord, forasmuch as ye know that your labor is not vain in the Lord" (1 Corinthians 15:58).

I ask God, in His keeping power, to keep me at the work. How else can I glorify Him? Jesus thought it right that lost men were to "see good works" in the lives of the disciples. He taught that these would glorify the Father who is in Heaven (Matthew 5:16). In the case of Jesus, His works brought glory to His Father. As He told His followers, when they begged Him to take time to eat: "My meat is to do the will of him that sent me, and to accomplish his work" (John 4:34).

Jesus set us the example of doing works of love for others. May He keep us from forgetting that "faith apart from works is dead" (James 2:26). May He show us God's design that our faith would be shown to others by our works (James 2:18).

There was nothing easy for Christ about His bearing the cross. Yet there are some so-called Christians who choose not to join a local congregation where they might be asked to do something, or to attend regularly, or to contribute to the support of the gospel. What a blessing they miss by dodging work.

This chapter has included a survey of Scripture texts where the word *kept* or *keep* is used. We have looked at passages where that word and idea have been seen in promises from God to us. We have found that God is our keeper. We have the warranty. There are wrongs *from* which He keeps us. We have been set *in* the way, where He keeps us. We have been given His word, *under* which He keeps us. And we have His work *at* which we ought to labor with our hands, not turning back.

Those who claim God's offered promise of security through time and eternity find they are kept in perfect peace "under His wings." Sit back and be buoyed up by the insight of William O. Cushing's song:

Under His wings I am safely abiding,
  Tho the night deepens and tempests are wild;
Still I can trust Him; I know He will keep me;
  He has redeemed me and I am His child.

Under His wings, what a refuge in sorrow!
  How the heart yearningly turns to His rest!
Often when earth has no balm for my healing,
  There I find comfort and there I am blest.

Under His wings, O what precious enjoyment!
  There will I hide till life's trials are o'er;
Sheltered, protected, no evil can harm me;
  Resting in Jesus I'm safe evermore.

Under His wings, under His wings,
  Who from His love can sever?
Under His wings my soul shall abide,
  Safely abide forever.

Thou Shalt Nots of Prayer

Thou shalt not faint
Thou shalt not fuss
Thou shalt not frown
Thou shalt not fret
Thou shalt not fear
Thou shalt not fail

9

The Promise of Prayer

When man speaks, does God listen? Does the maker of heaven and earth hear humans when they pray?

Doubters point to the great size of the universe. Believers point to the greatness of God. Skeptics say in ridicule that people who pray are simply talking with their eyes shut. Christians read with confidence the words of the psalmist: "He that planted the ear, shall he not hear? He that formed the eye, shall he not see?" (Psalm 94:9). The deniers of prayer's efficacy claim that for God to answer prayer would be too good to be true. People of faith exclaim that for the Lord to respond to human cries is too good not to be true.

Multitudes of believers are confident that God does answer prayer. George Buttrick says this is either the primary fact or the worst deception. There is no question as to what the Scriptures teach. The Bible promises in many places that "the eyes of Jehovah are toward the righteous, and his ears are open unto their cry" (Psalm 34:15).

What great privilege is granted to mortals! Anytime, anywhere, under any conditions, we can speak and God will hear us. Since God is God, He is omnipresent—He is there and sees our need. He is omniscient—He is sufficiently wise to know the solution to every dilemma. Having omnipotence, He is able to solve all problems. Being omniloving—all loving—He cares enough to act on our behalf. Nothing is impossible with such a Heavenly Father as Jesus revealed. Since God is God, it is impossible for the impossible to be impossible, and so Christians pray.

> Prayer is the key that opens heaven's door.
> Prayer brings us joy we never knew before.
> Learn how to pray; earth's shadows will depart.
> Prayer will bring Jesus into your heart.

Your copy of the Scripture contains instruction regarding prayer. It speaks of postures appropriate to prayer. It tells of people who prayed. It specifies types of prayer. It especially encourages people to pray more often than they do.

In your Bible you find that Jesus reminds people how the temple should be respected as "a house of prayer for all the nations" (Mark 11:17). In your Bible you read of Jesus' life of prayer. He prayed in upper rooms, in gardens like Gethsemane, and on mountaintops. He prayed everywhere. Those who pattern their lives after His find time to pray. It equally is true that churches following the standards set by New Testament believers give themselves to prayer. Pentecost came in A.D. 30, and the church was born. That church was preceded by prayer, permeated with prayer, and perpetuated by prayer. New Testament churches in every time of history are praying churches.

Reflecting on the Bible's teaching on prayer, it matters not if you stand in prayer, kneel in prayer, or lie prostrate in prayer; but it does matter that you talk with God. It is not essential that you bow your head, or close your eyes, or fold your hands in supplication; but it is of vital importance that you commune with the Lord and know that He answers prayer. (See Hebrews 11:6.)

If turns to *then* in the promise from Heaven. The promise states, "*If* my people, who are called by my name, shall humble themselves, and pray . . . *then* will I hear from heaven" (2 Chronicles 7:14). *If* disciples of Jesus "ask . . . seek . . . knock," *then* they receive, find, and enter doors that were closed (Matthew 7:7, 8).

As we explore the promise of prayer, so often heard throughout the entire Bible, let us look especially at a single chapter of the book of Philippians. We probe in chapter 4. At the center of this chapter are these words: "The Lord is at hand. In nothing be anxious; but in everything by prayer and supplication with thanksgiving let your requests be made known unto God" (verses 5, 6).

When Paul writes, "The Lord is at hand," he may be reminding us that Jesus' second coming is not too far away. But I think he is rather telling us that when we have a need, God is not so far removed from us that He is unaware of that need. He is "at hand," or close by, or near. When the followers of the Master call out for aid, their Lord is not so transcendent, not so far removed from earth, that He fails to hear their cry. "The Lord is at hand" to see the plight of His children and to hear the plea of their lips.

Read again the promise in its context: "The Lord is at hand. In nothing be anxious; but in everything by prayer and supplication with thanksgiving let your requests be made known unto God. And the peace of God, which passeth all understanding, shall guard your hearts and your thoughts in Christ Jesus" (Philippians 4:5-7).

See the confidence the apostle expresses regarding prayer. If Christians do not pray, they will be "anxious." If they do pray, their hearts will be guarded or garrisoned. They will know the indefinable "peace of God." Philippians 4:5-7 says so.

Notice with me the even larger context of our text from Philippians 4. To read verses 1-4 and 8-13 is to be learning still more about the topic of prayer. Paul not only uncovers the blessing of being freed from anxiety when we pray, but he also displays other benedictions that flow from prayer. Let us view these as well.

Thou Shalt Not Faint

The Old Covenant given at Mount Sinai contained commands that began "Thou shalt not." We are reading now what we might call some "thou shalt nots" of the New Covenant, but in Philippians 4 these are in the form of promises rather than commandments. Tie the idea of prayer to verse 1, and it may be considered a promise that if you pray "thou shalt not faint."

The text reads, "Wherefore, my brethren beloved and longed for, my joy and crown, so stand fast in the Lord, my beloved" (verse 1). I know from observation that those who "stand fast" in Christ are those who live in communion with Him through prayer.

Luke 18:1 records that Jesus "spake a parable unto them to the end that they ought always to pray, and not to faint." Those are the options He offered: pray or faint. If we keep on praying, we do not faint or fall. If we lose heart and fail in our praying, we lose strength and falter in other phases of our life. Keep communing with God, and "thou shalt not faint."

Jesus spoke of being the vine, with His disciples as the branches (John 15:1-8). In the intimate fellowship between vine and branches, all the sustenance needed by the disciples as branches comes from Jesus, "the true vine." He admonished the disciples to "abide" in Him (to have staying power and praying power), lest they be unfruitful. His words were, "Ask whatsoever ye will, and it shall be done unto you. Herein is my Father glorified, that ye bear much fruit" (John 15:7, 8). Abiding, praying, and bearing fruit rather than fainting, withering, and being cut away, is the result of intimate communion with Jesus.

You may have heard it said that "prayer ends sin, but sin ends prayer." If we pray steadfastly, we will not continue in sin—that is the way it works; but when we live in sin, we do cut back on prayer. The more consistently we maintain lives of prayer, the more certainly we will build holy and righteous character.

"He that endureth to the end, the same shall be saved" (Matthew 24:13). True enough! But what keeps a soul enduring? The strong hint, if not the ringing assertion, of the Scriptures, is that one's prayer life contributes to one's steadfastness. Those who pray do not faint. They "stand fast in the Lord" (Philippians 4:1).

Thou Shalt Not Fuss

I am glad Paul does not hide the trouble that existed in the Philippian congregation. Philippians 4:2, 3 names two women, Euodia and Syntyche, who had discordant views on some unnamed matter. Paul asks for help to be extended to these women by a "true yokefellow," who can yoke these dear souls together again.

Paul does not hide the trouble, but he proposes to end it. That may take the efforts of others as well as the two women who are involved in the dispute.

Sometimes we look back on the early church as if its members were living in a "golden age" when everything in the Lord's work went smoothly. The passage before us opens our eyes to see that congregations always have been made up of humans. This and other texts also help us see how praying people overcame their problems.

Paul speaks highly of these women. He points out that "they labored with me in the gospel." He seems confident that their names are in "the book of life" along with those of other fellow workers. He has no fear that his request for help will be rejected or that his plea "to be of the same mind in the Lord" will fall on deaf ears.

Swiftly he goes on to rejoicing, forbearance, and prayer (verses 4-6), knowing that this praying congregation will lift worthy requests before the Lord and that these praying women will be responsive to God's guidance.

We have seen that fainting is overcome by prayer. Now we see that fussing within the church body is overcome in the same way. When Jesus saw the possibility of division in the ranks of His followers, He went to prayer. He said to His Father, "I pray . . . that they may all be one" (John 17:20, 21). Apostles and the early church turned to prayer too.

The present-day Christian also has "fellow workers, whose names are in the book of life." If they sometimes get on said believer's nerves, it behooves him to stop and pray. Pray with John G. Whittier:

> Drop Thy still dews of quietness
>   Till all our strivings cease;
> Take from our souls the strain and stress,
> And let our ordered lives confess
>   The beauty of Thy peace.

Prayer helps us to live in harmony. Prayer changes things. Prayer changes the people for whom we pray. Best of all, prayer changes the people who do the praying. God is unchanging. Surely prayer moves Him to do what He would not do if no one cared enough to pray, but prayer's basic purpose is not to change God's mind or to bend His will to match ours. More properly it bends our will into harmony with His higher will. It leads the lips of man to plead, "Thy will be done."

Thou Shalt Not Frown

It is the will of God that His people not faint, nor fuss, nor frown. Prayer brings us into our Lord's way of thinking. Steadfastness, peace, and joy result. Verse 4 in our text from Philippians, chapter 4, is definite regarding the joy. "Rejoice in the Lord always: again I will say, Rejoice."

Why did Paul think it important to say, "Again I will say, Rejoice"? Was it because the people would be slow to believe that such an attitude of happiness was what Paul asked or his Savior wanted? How can a man writing from prison seem so full of gladness?

Remember that for four years the energetic missionary had been kept from his chosen task of opening new territory for the gospel. Two plus two is said to equal four. Two years in jail in Caesarea plus two years in Rome might be expected to add up to total sadness. But for this man of God there was no sadness. There should be none for the church he addressed.

"Rejoice in the Lord always." That is God's will in every circumstance. In reproach and persecution, God's own Son said the disciple is to "rejoice and be exceeding glad" (Matthew 5:11, 12). Jesus' brother so instructed those under his oversight. He wrote of the trials facing scattered Christians and instructed them to "count it all joy" (James 1:2-4). He added that, should they lack the wisdom to do this, their recourse was to "ask of God," and to "ask in faith" (James 1:5, 6). Praying in faith, nothing doubting, dispels gloom just as it disperses anger and weakness.

Youth choirs are heard to sing a little chorus beginning and ending, "I've got confidence." Our confidence is that God hears us when we pray. He helps us when we pray. He heartens us when we pray. He sees us through. It is not that we have total confidence in ourselves. We know that in our own strength we have nothing and are nothing. But we are certain that, because of the privilege of prayer, we have available the strength of God.

When the frowns start to come, we go to prayer. When a fuss begins, we call upon the Lord. When weakness comes over us and we commence to falter, we remember the promised strength available in communion with the Mighty One.

Thou Shalt Not Fret

We are ready to hear again some of the verses from Philippians 4. This time we commence with the beginning of verse 5. "Let your forbearance be known unto all men. The Lord is at hand. In nothing be anxious."

Anxiety, care, and worry are what John Wesley called "practical atheism." He meant that a man can talk about God constantly, and yet act as if no God existed. A person can insist that God reigns above, and yet turn only to his personal resources in the face of trouble. Such a one is a practical atheist, for he acts as if God were only a word and not a living person. To say, "I know God lives on high," but to believe you must solve all problems without divine aid, is to live like an atheist.

History tells that Martin Luther returned home one day to find his wife dressed in black garb, the attire worn when a person was in mourning. Luther asked her who had passed away. She replied, "God is dead." Martin rebuked her for such words. He made it clear that no mortal ever should speak that way about God. Then she reminded him that he was worrying as if God had died and all burdens had to be borne by Martin alone.

Had not Jesus taught, "Be not anxious for your life, what ye shall eat, or what ye shall drink; nor yet for your body, what ye shall put on"? Had He not insisted that His people on earth were of much more value than sparrows in the heavens or flowers of the field? The followers of the Messiah were to trust that their Heavenly Father knew their needs even before they asked (Matthew 6:25-34).

In spite of Jesus' insistence that His followers "be not therefore anxious" (Matthew 6:31), in spite of His assurance that the Heavenly Father gives "good things to them that ask him" (Matthew 7:11), in spite of the promise "every one that asketh receiveth" (Matthew 7:8), we catch ourselves getting overly concerned about certain matters. An unknown poet puts it thus:

> We mutter and sputter,
>   We fume and spurt,
> We mumble and grumble,
>   Our feelings get hurt;
> We can't understand things.
>   Our vision grows dim,
> When all that we need is
>   A moment with Him.

"In nothing be anxious; but in everything by prayer and supplication with thanksgiving let your requests be made known unto God" (Philippians 4:6).

Thou Shalt Not Fear

Verses 7 to 9 of Philippians 4 start with "the peace of God" and conclude with "the God of peace." Listen to the opening line: "And the *peace of God*, which passeth all understanding, shall guard your hearts and your thoughts in Christ Jesus."

With a heart garrisoned by God, there is no place for fear. A fortress surrounds us. We do not have to concern ourselves with enemies on the outside. Our minds do not need to focus on evil foes. We are secure in Christ to follow the apostolic words that are given:

> Finally, brethren, whatsoever things are true, whatsoever things are honorable, whatsoever things are just, whatsoever things are pure, whatsoever things are lovely, whatsoever things are of good report; if there be any virtue, and if there be any praise, think on these things. The things which ye both learned and received and heard and saw in me, these things do: and the *God of peace* shall be with you.

Communicate with God about the virtues Paul names. Share in quiet fellowship with the Father about the loveliness of character transparent in the life of His Son. Do this, and when you leave your quiet place, your upper room, your devotional closet, you will leave with "the peace of God."

The praying heart is the garrisoned heart. It shouts, "Whom shall I fear? . . . Of whom shall I be afraid?" (Psalm 27:1). It sings in dark shadows, "I will fear no evil; for thou art with me" (Psalm 23:4). All you who claim the promise of prayer, hear God's quiet, confident voice promise, "Thou shalt not fear." This is not to prohibit the proper fear of God, of course. That fear is the very beginning of wisdom (Psalm 111:10). But it is no part of wisdom to be tormented by other fears (1 John 4:18).

Those who fear the Lord—that is, those who hold God in awe, reverence, and respect—will not fear or have a phobia about the cares of the world. A magnificent psalm becomes a paean of praise as it invites, "Let them now that fear Jehovah say that his lovingkindness endureth for ever. . . . Jehovah is on my side; I will not fear: what can man do unto me?" (Psalm 118:4, 6).

Thou Shalt Not Fail

With the theme of prayer in mind, we take a final look into the last chapter of Philippians. This time we read verses 10-13. The gist of Paul's words is that in every circumstance he knows he will not fail with Christ's strengthening.

He expresses joy that his friends at Philippi have sent him aid. He mentions his want, but also his ability to be content in any state or condition. Then he says,

> I know how to be abased, and I know also how to abound: in everything and in all things have I learned the secret both to be filled and to be hungry, both to abound and to be in want. I can do all things in him that strengtheneth me.

You have heard the bottom line. Paul "can do all things" through Christ. He can successfully face either prosperity or penury. Intimate fellowship with his Lord makes him victor. All who have that same close prayer-relationship with God have spiritual ears that hear Him promise, "Thou shalt not fail."

"I can do all things through him" is the believer's confidence. How can you and I turn the "I can" of this sentence to an "I will"? How can we turn our latent faith into active trust? We must make the effort to pray continually until our personal words are "I will do the task before me. I believe I can succeed in facing financial hardship or fiscal fluency as a Christian ought. I am determined, by praying for God's help, that I will be Christian in every attitude. I will try and I will succeed, for I know that those who persistently pray will not fail."

The prodigal, in the story Jesus told, did not say, "I can go back home to my father's house some day." He was more decisive. He said, "I will arise and go to my father, and will say unto him, Father . . . make me as one of thy hired servants" (Luke 15:18, 19).

I call your attention to the change in the prayer life of the prodigal. Luke 15 records his two prayers. One prayer was made when he was leaving home and striving to get as far from his father as he could possibly go. The other prayer was uttered as he longed to get all the way back where he belonged.

Prayer number one was "Give me!" "Give me the portion of thy substance that falleth to me" (Luke 15:12). That is the sound that comes from the lips of persons who are far from the real purpose and meaning of prayer.

Prayer number two comes after learning life's lesson. The sincere heart's cry is now, "Make me . . . a servant." From "give me" to "make me" is a tremendous distance in spiritual miles. Through Christ's help as we pray, we can make the pilgrimage. You and I "can do all things in him," if we will.

This study of the prayer promise has caused us to hear words from "Thou shalt not faint" to "Thou shalt not fail." We should hear one more Heavenly word. It is that, knowing of the value of prayer, we are to increase the practice of it. "Thou shalt not hesitate."

I know not by what methods rare,
But this I know, God answers prayer.
I know that He has given His word
That tells me prayer is always heard
And will be answered soon or late,
And so I pray and calmly wait.
I know not if the blessing sought
Will come in just the way I thought,
But I leave my prayers with Him alone
Whose will is wiser than my own,
Assured that He will grant my quest
Or send some answer far more blest.

10

He Leadeth Me

out of bondage
over mountains
through deserts
into the promised land

10

The Promise of Guidance

Jehovah is my shepherd; I shall not want. He maketh me to lie down in green pastures; he leadeth me beside still waters. He restoreth my soul: he guideth me in the paths of righteousness for his name's sake. Yea, though I walk through the valley of the shadow of death, I will fear no evil; for thou art with me; thy rod and thy staff, they comfort me. Thou preparest a table before me in the presence of mine enemies: thou hast anointed my head with oil; my cup runneth over. Surely goodness and lovingkindness shall follow me all the days of my life; and I shall dwell in the house of Jehovah for ever.

—Psalm 23:1-6

This beloved Twenty-third Psalm has been a favorite to Israel, a favorite to the church, a favorite to all. The phrases "He leadeth me" and "He guideth me" caused Jews to remember how God had guided their nation from Egyptian bondage, through wilderness wanderings, and into the promised land.

Christians found the Lord to be their shepherd, guiding them as the new "Israel of God" (Galatians 6:16), the New Covenant "twelve tribes" (James 1:1), the modern "sojourners" (1 Peter 1:1). As Paul reasoned, "he is not a Jew who is one outwardly; neither is that circumcision which is outward in the flesh: but he is a Jew who is one inwardly; and circumcision is that of the heart" (Romans 2:28, 29). Whether he is Jew or Gentile, one who becomes a Christian is guided out of his bondage to sin, through the rest of his life on earth, and into the promised land of Heaven.

Individuals from many religious backgrounds, coming into the Christian faith, have found Jesus' words to be true: "I am the good shepherd: the good shepherd layeth down his life for the sheep" (John 10:11).

Psalm 23 ministers to the heart because it pictures God as one who leads His people, cares for them, and tends them in every need. The psalm also rightly describes man as a being in need of such care and guidance. King David's words realistically paint a picture of life as having grievous perils between its "green pastures" and the golden portals. Occasionally there is "the valley of the shadow," "the presence of . . . enemies" and frightening "evil."

It will do us good to examine this ancient Shepherd Psalm and bathe our minds in the refreshing promise of God's guidance.

He Leadeth Out of Bondage

If at the present time we find ourselves able to "lie down in green pastures," enjoy "still waters," and know "the paths of righteousness," we need to remember that neither we nor the ancient Israelites always had these blessings.

Review an Old Testament story, for it was recorded for the profit of believers in New Testament times. Paul saw what happened at the exodus of Israel from Egypt to be a type of God's deliverance today. He wrote, "Now these things were our examples" (1 Corinthians 10:6) and "they were written for our admonition, upon whom the ends of the ages are come" (verse 11).

He began the tenth chapter of 1 Corinthians thus:

> For I would not, brethren, have you ignorant, that our fathers were all under the cloud, and all passed through the sea; and were all baptized unto Moses in the cloud and in the sea.
> —1 Corinthians 10:1, 2

He meant that all who today find Christ as the Good Shepherd have undergone a deliverance parallel to Israel's deliverance. They had been slaves in Egypt. They had been in bondage to Pharaoh, but God had intervened and set them free.

We had a past when we lived in sin. Satan was our taskmaster. But, praise be to God, we have been delivered. Paul reminded his Christian readers,

> Know ye not, that to whom ye present yourselves as servants unto obedience, his servants ye are whom ye obey; whether of sin unto death, or of obedience unto righteousness? But thanks be to God, that, whereas ye were servants of sin, ye became obedient from the heart to that form of teaching whereunto ye were delivered; and being made free from sin, ye became servants of righteousness.
>
> —Romans 6:16-18

Not always have we been free. Not always have we walked in righteous paths. Once all of those now called "saints" were known as "sinners." We have been delivered. As the woman taken in adultery found grace in Christ and not condemnation, we are told at our forgiveness, "Neither do I condemn thee: go thy way; from henceforth sin no more" (John 8:11). "For freedom did Christ set us free"; we are not to be "entangled again in a yoke of bondage" (Galatians 5:1). "If . . . the Son shall make you free, ye shall be free indeed" (John 8:36).

In Israel's deliverance at the exodus, the Red Sea played an important part. God parted the waters. Israel marched to freedom with a wall of water on either side and a cloud covering them from above. The Egyptian army followed them into the sea, only to find that the waters closed over Pharaoh's soldiers and they were drowned.

Paul makes that part of the deliverance story a parallel to Christian baptism (1 Corinthians 10:1, 2). On one side of baptism Satan was our leader and kept us in bondage. On the other side of baptism Christ has become our leader and has set us free. Before the deliverance there were Pharaoh and Egypt, the types of Satan and sin. After the rescue there were Moses and freedom, the symbols of Christ and salvation. The sea was the dividing line between Pharaoh's leadership and that of Moses. Baptism is that visible dividing line between Satan's mastery and Jesus' lordship. "For as many of you as were baptized into Christ did put on Christ" (Galatians 3:27).

That deliverance from bondage in ancient Egypt was connected with the blood of the Passover lamb shed and applied. Jesus became the "Lamb of God" (John 1:36; 1 Corinthians 5:7), whose blood is essential to man's deliverance.

He Leadeth Over Mountains

Those delivered from sin's slavery are grateful that God leads them out of bondage. The redeemed are filled with thanksgiving that God's promise of guidance includes also His leading beyond that point. He leads those who belong to Him over mountains of difficulty and alpine hills of obstacle.

Delivered Israel found the Lord's guidance leading them all the way to the promised land. There were forty years between escape from Egypt and crossing the Jordan. There may be many years between our baptism and our entrance into Heaven. We need God's guidance each step of the way.

What do we do when we find "tribulation" (John 16:33) or discover that "straitened" is "the way, that leadeth unto life"? (Matthew 7:14). Where do we turn when, as the gospel chorus suggests, rivers seem uncrossable and there are mountains we can't tunnel through? We are to remember "God specializes in things thought impossible; He does the things others cannot do."

Faith in Christ sometimes moves mountains of difficulty (Matthew 17:20; 21:21; 1 Corinthians 13:2). At other times, when the mountain of trouble doesn't vanish, faith brings Christ's strength to help us scale the obstacle in our way.

Let's name a few mountains that may rise in your path. A Christian can lose his job. He will need Christ's guidance. A believer can lose a friend. Jesus did. The third year of His ministry is often called "the intensive year of opposition." It immediately followed "the popular year of public favor." John records that "many of his [Christ's] disciples went back, and walked no more with him" (John 6:66). If a friend leaves you, you will need the "friend that sticketh closer than a brother" (Proverbs 18:24) to lead and guide.

A disciple of Jesus can lose his life. He may lose it at an unseemly time, and in an unfortunate way. Whether death comes from natural causes or martyrdom, when the Lord shepherds the soul it will "fear no evil" even in "the valley of the shadow of death" (Psalm 23:4).

A faithful evangelist can lose his health. Timothy, Trophimus, Epaphroditus, and others can attest to that (1 Timothy 5:23; 2 Timothy 4:20; Philippians 2:25-27). But when troubles are there, rest assured that our shepherd is there as well.

Having the divine promise that the Good Shepherd leads His sheep, we follow unafraid. We admonish our brothers with this stanza from an unknown author:

Press on. Surmount the rocky steeps.
  Climb boldly o'er the torrent's arch.
He fails alone who feebly creeps.
  He wins who dares the hero's march.

He Leadeth Through Deserts

Have you noticed that sometimes the path before you is not leading to a challenging mountain that dares you to conquer it? What lies before you is more comparable to desert.

Life has lost its excitement. What is ahead for you appears to be arid, dry, boring. It is "blah" as far as your eyes can see. Soldiers in World War I could sing, "It's a long, long way to Tipperary." In your daily battle it looks like it will be "a far piece" through the daily routine to some oasis in your desert.

Jesus, our leader and guide, knows about such times and conditions. He knew the thrilling moment of His anointing. At His baptism in the Jordan, the Heavenly Father's voice broke the silence with the words, "This is my beloved Son, in whom I am well pleased" (Matthew 3:17), and the Holy Spirit descended upon Him. Yet the next incident that Matthew records after this climactic experience is forty days of desert, wilderness, and temptation.

The inner circle of the apostolic band knew the highest of mountaintop experiences. Somewhere on a high mountain they saw Jesus transfigured before their eyes. They beheld Moses and Elijah talking with Christ, and they heard God's voice "out of the cloud, saying, This is my beloved Son, in whom I am well pleased; hear ye him" (Matthew 17:1-8). Yet here we find an unequalled, awe-inspiring experience followed in the very same chapter by a discouraging failure on the part of nine disciples (Matthew 17:14-21).

On the day after the disciples saw Jesus glorified, they found fellow apostles failing. On the day after they heard the Father say, "I am well pleased" (verse 5), they heard the Son say, "O faithless and perverse generation, how long shall I be with you?" (verse 17).

I have received phone calls from young preachers sharing their thrill of receiving calls to serve their first congregations. I have taken other calls in the late night hours from brokenhearted young ministers who have been asked to leave their particular work for God.

You perhaps have shared the joys of a young couple beginning life together. You may have felt their hurts, when for some mysterious reason "the honeymoon was over."

All the happy and the brokenhearted have one certainty. That assurance, like a bright star, shines into the dark night. God leads through deserts. He leads all the way through.

Several things impress me in the middle of David's psalm. One is the preposition *through*. One is the pronoun *thou*. And one is *death*, called "the valley of the shadow."

If there is shade or shadow in the valley, it is because there is sunlight on the other side of the mountain. That implies that the time of death has its darkness, but on the other side of death there is glorious light.

The psalmist in his first three verses used the third-person pronoun. He talked about God and how He led, how He restored, how He guided. At verse 4, the verse of death, he talks no longer *about* his Lord. He now talks *to* Him: "*Thou* art with me." Death places us in Jehovah's very presence. We who have talked about Him may now talk with Him face to face.

But look now at David's exciting choice of the specific preposition *through*. When we go into the dark and shadowy vale of death there would be fear if that were the end of the journey. But it is not! Our shepherd does not lead any of His sheep *into* death, *into* a valley that is a dead end. He leads every lamb and every old sheep *through* that valley to the other side. There we "shall dwell in the house of Jehovah for ever" (verse 6).

For forty long years Israel had God's pillar of fire to guide them through the dark nights. For all of those years they had their shepherd lead them through the days by a pillar of cloud.

"Fear not the things which thou art about to suffer" (Revelation 2:10). He who tends Heaven's flock will lead you through.

He Leadeth Into the Promised Land

"I shall dwell in the house of Jehovah for ever" (Psalm 23:6). Of that same "house" Jesus spoke when He said, "In my Father's house are many mansions . . . I go to prepare a place for you" (John 14:2). To that same house Jesus made reference in the conclusion of his Prodigal Son story. That house of Heaven is filled with music when sinners come home (Luke 15:7, 10, 25).

The end of Israel's long journey was Canaan. The river Jordan finally was crossed, and each wanderer could settle down under his own vine and fig tree. Permanent homes could replace tents. They had arrived!

The Christian "crosses over Jordan" at death. The land beyond the river flows with milk and honey. Canaan was a dim picture of our eternal homeland. But like Israel of old, in this life we are "strangers and pilgrims" (Hebrews 11:13). We sing, "This world is not my home, I'm just a-passing through." We look for "the city which hath the foundations, whose builder and maker is God" (Hebrews 11:10). We "desire a better country, that is, a heavenly [land]" (verse 16).

> I've reached the land of corn and wine,
> And all its riches freely mine . . .
> I look away across the sea,
> Where mansions are prepared for me,
> And view the shining glory shore—
> My heav'n, my home for evermore.
> —Edgar Page

Are you bound for the promised land of eternity? In typology, Jacob's offspring were led out of Egyptian bondage over perilous mountains and through oppressive deserts, but finally into the promised land. In fulfillment of that picture-prophecy of type and shadow is the New Testament story of Christian deliverance.

Some of the examples Paul found in the parallel between Israel's rescue from Egypt and the church's deliverance from sin may now be personalized.

Am I out of Egypt or still in it? Are you looking *back* on your baptism into Christ or *forward* to it? Are we started on the journey? Are we staying on the journey toward Heaven? Can you and I say with David, "Jehovah is my shepherd," emphasizing the second and third words? It is essential to my salvation that Jehovah is *my* shepherd. It is basic to each man's security that he be able to speak of a present status and not just one past and gone. He must state the present reality: "Jehovah is my shepherd . . . He leadeth me . . . He guideth me."

To such as hear Christ's voice and follow Him, He gives eternal life; and they shall never perish, and no one shall snatch them out of His hand (John 10:27, 28). It is true of Christ's flock that they were going astray like sheep; but are now returned unto the Shepherd and Bishop of their souls (1 Peter 2:25). God's promise of guidance has seen to that.

The Promise of

D edication
I nstruction
S hepherding
C orrection
I ntercession
P ardon
L ove
I nclusion
N earness
E ncouragement

11

The Promise of Discipline

The book of Proverbs is filled with promises. Its third chapter is no exception. Proverbs 3 contains promises I like, I need, and I want.

Verses 5 and 6 contain the familiar words, "Trust in Jehovah with all thy heart, and lean not upon thine own understanding: in all thy ways acknowledge him, and he will direct thy paths." I need that assurance. I want that which is promised.

Verses 9 and 10 encourage the reader with another commitment: "Honor Jehovah with thy substance, and with the first-fruits of all thine increase: so shall thy barns be filled with plenty, and thy vats shall overflow with new wine." I like that promise too. I need to hear its words of hope. I want that promise as well.

But verses 11 and 12 contain a promise I am not so sure I want. The words are, "My son, despise not the chastening of Jehovah; neither be weary of his reproof: for whom Jehovah loveth he reproveth, even as a father the son in whom he delighteth." The book of Hebrews quotes this promise as reading, "My son, regard not lightly the chastening of the Lord, nor faint when thou art reproved of him; for whom the Lord loveth he chasteneth, and scourgeth every son whom he receiveth" (Hebrews 12:5, 6).

My first reaction—the "off-the-top-of-the-head" response—is that I do not want such a promise. I do not desire to be disciplined. But after thinking about it, I am sure I want this promise too.

The word *chastening* or *discipline* does not always connote stripes, punishment, or the wrath of God. The Greek word *paideuo* describes the training of a child at home and school. *Pais,* the root word in *paideuo,* means son or child. I do want, as a child of God, to have the training He promises to "every son whom he receiveth."

Child-training, or son-rearing, is offered by the Father to all whom He loves. His tender discipline is to make us everything He wants us to be. I first thought of what many refer to as "a razor-strap experience in the woodshed," and that led me to doubt that I would like this promised discipline. The fuller awareness of what is truly included reverses my first reaction. That our Father disciplines does not suggest that He is harsh or heartless. It affirms that He cares and loves.

True, discipline is sometimes unpleasant. The word *scourgeth* makes that plain. Hebrews 12:11 says, "All chastening seemeth for the present to be not joyous but grievous; yet afterward it yieldeth peaceable fruit unto them that have been exercised thereby, even the fruit of righteousness." Even if discipline is painful, I want it because of what comes afterward.

Christians are commonly called *disciples*. That is the name given to Jesus' followers more than any other in the New Testament. *Disciple* and *discipline* go together. Every disciple is under the discipline of the Master. The student selects his teacher, desiring to become like him. Therefore he subjects himself to the discipline required.

We correctly call the Bible our book of discipline. Christ is our headmaster. He changes our thinking and our lives by His teaching that is found in the Bible, especially in the New Testament.

Examine with me this promise we all need and we all ought to want. It is a promise that contains within itself many other promises. Allow me to uncover ten such promises within the discipline promise. Permit me to point out the subpromises with the aid of an acrostic on the word *discipline*. We'll look at these two at a time.

Dedication and Instruction

The church's instruction is to "make disciples . . . baptizing them," according to Matthew 28:19. The participle *baptizing* describes how disciples are made. The act of baptism is the act of enrollment into the school of Christ. That is where there is the teaching of all Christ commanded (verse 20). The word *disciples* means learners. Christ's disciples learn in His church.

The baptism of a believer is a covenant-like pledge, or contract, between the pupil and the teacher. As in any college-level course, it is understood in the act of enrollment that the teacher is promising to give the student some time and attention. The pupil is committing himself to carry out the assignments so that he will gain the intended benefits of the experience.

At the very root of the idea of discipline is the concept of mutual dedication. In the Christian context, you and I dedicate ourselves to be Christ's followers. He dedicates himself to see us through the training successfully.

In ideal parenting, the father and mother recognize the responsibility that is theirs. Having brought a child into the world, they have a responsibility to that child. Whatever the sacrifice, being a mother or a father requires more than reproduction. It demands dedicated care and guidance through the years. God thought of that before He made us His children.

Being the citizen of a country illustrates in another way the two-sided relationship of discipline. The nation has responsiblities to its citizens. The people of a country have responsibilities to their homeland. Each pledges allegiance to the other. All discipline starts with such dedication.

We who are in God's family, we who are citizens of the kingdom of Heaven, we who have enrolled as Christ's disciples, are overwhelmed by the Lord's commitment to those who constitute His church. Review His promises of dedication in passages like John 10:28, Romans 8:38, 39, and Hebrews 13:5. Christ is committed to His people. He is dedicated to their development as Christians.

As Matthew 28:19, 20 implies, God's dedication to you and me as disciples is a commitment to our instruction in the way of the Lord. The textbook for our development is the "scripture inspired of God." The sacred writings are "profitable for teaching, for reproof, for correction, for instruction" (2 Timothy 3:16). The word *instruction* here is the word *discipline*. It is so translated in some versions of the New Testament and in the footnotes of the *American Standard Version*. It is the same word that is translated *chastening* in Hebrews 12:5.

Along with the concept of being a disciple is the imagery of sitting at the feet of Jesus the Master Teacher for instruction. As we read of the first disciples, it is true also of us: "When he [Jesus] had sat down, his disciples came unto him: and he opened his mouth and taught them" (Matthew 5:1, 2).

Shepherding and Correction

God's discipline implies His dedication and His instruction to those He disciplines. It assures as well His shepherding and His correction.

A good shepherd does far more than feed his flock. He pastors them. The Christ who gave to the church "some to be apostles; and some prophets; and some, evangelists," also gave "some, pastors and teachers" (Ephesians 4:11). Note the conjunction *and*. Pastoring and teaching may be done by the same person, but they are two facets of the ministry. Both are equally vital. In addition to a believer's need to be taught is his need to be guided, encouraged, helped, protected. In a word, he needs to be *shepherded*. The Greek word for *pastor* literally means a shepherd.

How blessed is the Sunday-school class that, in addition to lessons taught, finds shepherding taking place! How certain of God's favor is the congregation with a leadership concerned not only for what is taught from the pulpit, but also for the pastoring needed by the flock! How helped in understanding his ministry was Peter, when Jesus asked him not only to "feed my lambs," but also to "tend my sheep" (John 21:15, 16). *Tend* represents the work of elders. As overseers or bishops, they are to "feed the church of the Lord" (Acts 20:28). The *American Standard Version* here translates *poimaino* with the limited word *feed*. The Greek word is much richer in meaning. It is inclusive of the entire shepherd's task, and that is more than simply feeding his flock. The shepherd leads the sheep from place to place (Psalm 23:2); he gives special care to any that are hurt or sick; he protects from danger (1 Samuel 17:34, 35); he is gentle with pregnant ewes and he carries young lambs in his bosom (Isaiah 40:11).

As the Good Shepherd made clear, when even one sheep strays away from a large flock the shepherd is more than an unconcerned hireling. True pastoring demands that he "go after that which is lost, until he find it" (Luke 15:4). Since some spiritual shepherds in Jesus' day forgot that their mission was to do more than expound in the synagogues, Christ felt compassion for the people, saying they were "as sheep not having a shepherd" (Matthew 9:36).

Each teacher, each preacher, each youth worker, each elder needs to test his work with the people entrusted to him. Is there only teaching? Or is the instruction accompanied with a shepherding that goes after the absentee? Now turn this thought around. While we should be concerned about those in our care, we ought to rejoice in the promise we are studying just now. Christ's discipline promise includes His pledge to shepherd us.

We often sing Elizabeth C. Clephane's song that Ira D. Sankey set to music. Right now, read every line slowly and ponder the cost to Christ in being your shepherd.

> There were ninety and nine that safely lay
>   In the shelter of the fold,
> But one was out on the hills away,
>   Far off from the gates of gold—
> Away on the mountains wild and bare,
> Away from the tender Shepherd's care.
>
> "Lord, Thou hast here Thy ninety and nine;
>   Are they not enough for Thee?"
> But the Shepherd made answer: "This of mine
>   Has wandered away from me;
> And although the road be rough and steep,
> I go to the desert to find my sheep."
>
> But none of the ransomed ever knew
>   How deep were the waters crossed;
> Nor how dark was the night that the Lord passed thro'
>   Ere He found His sheep that was lost.
> Out in the desert He heard its cry—
> Sick and helpless, and ready to die.
>
> "Lord, whence are those blood-drops all the way
>   That mark out the mountain's track?"
> "They were shed for one who had gone astray
>   Ere the Shepherd could bring him back."
> "Lord, whence are Thy hands so rent and torn?"
> "They're pierced tonight by many a thorn."
>
> But all thro' the mountains, thunder-riven,
>   And up from the rocky steep,
> There arose a glad cry to the gate of heaven,
>   "Rejoice! I have found my sheep!"
> And the angels echoed around the throne,
>   "Rejoice, for the Lord brings back His own!"

If shepherding of this nature is a part of discipline, then I want God's discipline. At the ordination of ministers to carry on the work of discipling, 2 Timothy 4:1, 2 generally is read. It starts, "I charge thee in the sight of God. . . ." It continues, "reprove, rebuke, exhort. . . ." That is the part of God's assignment that I at first did not like to hear. That is a part of God's promised discipline that at first I questioned.

The child may not like being patted on the back, when the patting is "low enough and hard enough" to bring correction. But later the child will be glad for it.

Do you pay a music teacher for lessons that do not correct your errors, timing, or wrist motion? Will you study English from an instructor who fails to make any correction of mistakes in punctuation, spelling, or style? Would being Jesus' disciple have value if He did not correct us when we go wrong?

The helpful, brotherly way of disciples of Christ is this: "If thy brother sin, rebuke him; and if he repent, forgive him" (Luke 17:3). Guiding principles for disciplinary action are clearly set forth in Matthew 18:15-18. When a brother sins, you are to go to him alone. Only if repentance does not come is another one or two to help. And only as a last resort is the whole church to be informed and asked to act. The purpose is not retribution but rescue. A brother overtaken in a trespass is to be weaned from the world and tied to the Savior. It is brotherly to help.

The Corinthian Christians, as an act of discipline, put a man out of their fellowship. Unrepentant, he had indulged in "such fornication as is not even among the Gentiles" (1 Corinthians 5:1). Under Paul's guidance, they treated the man as no longer a Christian (1 Corinthians 5:3-5, 13). Their kind but firm action was seen to be the hand of love drawing the erring brother back. To be willing to share in such a congregational action is a part of the covenant the disciple makes. No Christian can fall away from Christ's way without having the family members try to stop such a tragedy.

Intercession and Pardon

Discipline is a flower of ten petals. All of them say, "He loves me." None of them say, "He loves me not." Intercession is one of the petals of promise.

Christ prays for me as His disciple. He intercedes with the Father on my behalf. "Wherefore also he is able to save to the uttermost them that draw near unto God through him, seeing he ever liveth to make intercession for them" (Hebrews 7:25). He can save to the uttermost, and from the guttermost, because He intercedes.

Christ's intercession with the Father is paralleled by the Spirit's intercession.

> In like manner the Spirit also helpeth our infirmity: for we know not how to pray as we ought; but the Spirit himself maketh intercession for us with groanings which cannot be uttered; and he that searcheth the hearts knoweth what is the mind of the Spirit, because he maketh intercession for the saints according to the will of God.
> —Romans 8:26, 27

As if that were not enough, the church is called upon to join in intercession: "I exhort therefore, first of all, that supplications, prayers, intercessions, thanksgivings, be made for all men" (1 Timothy 2:1). "Pray one for another" (James 5:16).

"Ere you left your room this morning, did you think to pray?" Praying for others is a part of discipleship. Can you assure others, "For you I am praying, for you I am praying, for you I am praying, I'm praying for you"?

When in our shepherding it is necessary to do any correcting, it must be evident to those corrected that we are interceding for them and are ready to pardon and accept them back.

As Paul had ordered the Corinthians to break fellowship with the incestuous brother, he admonished them to embrace him when he gave up his sin. Paul wrote, "Ye should rather forgive him and comfort him, lest by any means such a one should be swallowed up with his overmuch sorrow . . . confirm your love toward him" (2 Corinthians 2:7, 8). It must be that way, for we pray, "Forgive us our debts, as we also have forgiven our debtors" (Matthew 6:12). It must be that way, for we have the apostolic admonition, "Be ye kind one to another, tenderhearted, forgiving each other, even as God also in Christ forgave you" (Ephesians 4:32).

Love and Inclusion

Upon correcting others and upon interceding for those being corrected, there is the additional need for reaching out to pardon the penitent upon his coming home. Love and inclusion are basic elements of the ministry of discipline. If anyone is put out of the church for sin, or if anyone feels out of God's grace because of guilt, such a one may be so crushed by grief that he will never come back. That is, he may not return unless he knows that love awaits him in God's house.

Perhaps you remember the speech that your mother or father gave you when you were very little and discipline became necessary: "This hurts me more than it hurts you." That was hard to believe then, but it became undoubtable later, when tender arms held you and tear-filled eyes brimmed over with liquid love.

Isaiah could not contain his gratitude: "I will make mention of the lovingkindnesses of Jehovah. . . . For he said, Surely, they are my people, children that will not deal falsely: so he was their Saviour. In all their affliction he was afflicted" (Isaiah 63:7-9). Our pains are His pains. God is love, and loving opens the lover to hurts.

Discipline never works unless love and inclusion are there. A child receiving a spanking is made a better child only when he or she feels the love more than the pain.

Nearness and Encouragement

If we had a vote on whether to accept God's promise of disciplining those He loves, we would vote no if we failed to see all the love that is included. Our analysis of the promise of discipline has uncovered ten other promises always present when God fulfills this promise. We have called to our aid an acrostic to help us see the many facets of this great blessing.

The *D* in *discipline* calls to mind Christ's dedication to our maturing in the faith. The *I* brings to remembrance His instruction that guides our feet. *S* points to His shepherding concern. *C* promises that He will correct us when we sin, for He cares what we become. *I* speaks of His intercession before the Father on our behalf. *P* pledges pardon the moment we turn toward him. *L* reminds of the love that is always there. *I* paints the picture of His outstretched inclusive arms ready to receive us. The final letters *N* and *E* cap the altar of gratitude erected for His name. *N* is for His nearness when we need Him, and *E* is for the encouragement He gives.

The promise etched in the New Testament reads, "Draw nigh to God, and he will draw nigh to you" (James 4:8). The promise inscribed in the Old Covenant says, "Jehovah is nigh unto all them that call upon him" (Psalm 145:18). What assurance calms the souls that realize "God is our refuge and strength, a very present help in trouble"! (Psalm 46:1).

Christ specializes in encouraging His disciples. "A bruised reed will he not break, and a dimly burning wick will he not quench" (Isaiah 42:3).

> We have not a high priest that cannot be touched with the feeling of our infirmities; but one that has been in all points tempted like as we are, yet without sin. Let us therefore draw near with boldness unto the throne of grace, that we may receive mercy, and may find grace to help us in time of need.
> —Hebrews 4:15, 16

It is upbuilding to hear again what we realize already. We know that Christ is "touched with the feeling of our infirmities." That being true, Christlikeness in all of His followers ought to include encouragement to others. To be people of encouragement is the Heavenly command of Hebrews 10:24: "Let us consider one another to provoke unto love and good works." *Provoke* in this Scripture means to stir up or to encourage. You may not have the name of Barnabas, but you will be a needed blessing if you have his ministry. *Barnabas* means *son of encouragement.*

Why does God promise to discipline? The Bible answer is this:

> God dealeth with you as with sons. . . . We had the fathers of our flesh to chasten us, and we gave them reverence: shall we not much rather be in subjection unto the Father of spirits, and live? For they indeed for a few days chastened us as seemed good to them; but he for our profit, that we may be partakers of his holiness. All chastening seemeth for the present to be not joyous but grievous; yet afterward it yieldeth peaceable fruit unto them that have been exercised thereby, even the fruit of righteousness. Wherefore lift up the hands that hang down, and the palsied knees; and make straight paths for your feet, that that which is lame be not turned out of the way, but rather be healed.
> —Hebrews 12:7-13

Is that what I want? Knowing that God's disciplining me means God cares for me, I want it because I need it. When I was a young father I did not run around the community and spank every child in town. (On a few occasions, I do recall feeling like it.) But I limited my discipline to the ones I really cared about—my very own children. God's discipline is wonderful because it means those disciplined are in His family. You and I mean something very special to God.

God is the Heavenly Father. The church is called "our mother" (Galatians 4:26) and has a share in the loving ministry of discipline. The purpose of all disciplining in the church is to bring the erring children back so that not one will perish.

We need to have evangelistic concern. New brothers and sisters are welcome in this family. But equally we need to concern ourselves for every person that has entered our local fellowship in the past. To bring all the family back together is the outcome of discipline and its aim. Not one is to be allowed to slip away. God cares about that. So should we. "We are chastened of the Lord, that we may not be condemned with the world" (1 Corinthians 11:32). That is a promise.

12

The Promise of Return

How?
  the manner
Why?
  the purpose
When?
  the time
What?
  the preparation

12

The Promise of Christ's Return

We have the promise that Christ will return to this earth. This "promise of his coming" (2 Peter 3:4) is a hope-building promise. It is worthy of deliberate thought.

Do we ask, "Till what point in time are we to continue observing the Lord's Supper?" The Bible answer is, "Till he come" (1 Corinthians 11:26). Do we inquire how long we are to continue evangelizing? The Scriptural reply is, "Unto the end of the world" (Matthew 28:20), which is the same as saying "until Jesus comes." Do we wonder at what point in history the gospel age will close? The response of God's Word is that it will close when Jesus comes again. He "shall appear a second time, apart from sin, to them that wait for him, unto salvation" (Hebrews 9:28). That is a promise.

> I saw a youth with soul aflame,
> As to life's parting ways he came,
> Pause for a moment to behold
> The glittering pleasures of sin's gold;
> But then he firmly grasped the cross
> And counted all of earth as dross.
> His aged father urged him on
> And said, "Be faithful still, my son,
>   Till Jesus comes."

I saw a missionary stand
Upon a foreign ocean strand.
His eyes looked back to home and friends;
His heart looked forward to earth's ends.
With perils of the deep before,
With perils of the foreign shore,
His lips the words repeated o'er:
> "Till Jesus comes."

I saw a lonely woman stand
With empty heart and idle hand
Beside a mound upon a hill—
A lonely spot, so calm and still.
She thought of happy days lived o'er;
She thought of lonely years before,
With courage saying evermore,
> "Till Jesus comes."

O precious words! How much they hold
For young and strong, for weak and old!
From manhood's golden hours of youth
To sorrow's search for hope and truth,
From dawn of day to setting sun,
From earth's bright hours till life is done,
May we be faithful every one
> Till Jesus comes.
>> —Author Unknown

Back in the gold-rush days in California, a man came from the East hoping to strike it rich. He dreamed of making life easier for his wife and children, whom he had left behind for a time. To let them know he still thought of them, he sent letters and gifts regularly.

As many months passed, the loved ones wrote again and again to express appreciation for the correspondence and gifts; but they ended almost every letter with the plea, "We miss you. We thank you for the letters and gifts, but we miss you—come home."

So the Christian's heart calls out to Jesus with gratitude for His New Testament "love letters" and His daily gifts, but ends with the closing cry of "Come, Lord Jesus" (Revelation 22:20).

The second coming of Christ receives prime time in the New Testament. It is said to be mentioned nearly three hundred times. I have not counted them myself, but I am sure the number of them is more than sufficient.

Jesus himself spoke often of His return. In the upper room the night before He died, He addressed His intimate followers with this assurance:

> Let not your heart be troubled: believe in God, believe also in me. In my Father's house are many mansions; if it were not so, I would have told you; for I go to prepare a place for you. And if I go and prepare a place for you, I come again, and will receive you unto myself; that where I am, there ye may be also.
> —John 14:1-3

That promise given before the crucifixion was underscored to the apostles at the ascension. "Two men . . . in white apparel" brought the message. Most students agree that these were angels from Heaven. They said,

> Ye men of Galilee, why stand ye looking into heaven? this Jesus, who was received up from you into heaven, shall so come in like manner as ye beheld him going into heaven.
> —Acts 1:11

This text begins to suggest an answer to the questions in the heart of every believer as he meditates on the promise of Christ's return. How will the King return? Why? When? What must we do to be ready for that glad day?

The Manner of His Coming

"This Jesus . . . shall so come in like manner." He will come as He went when He ascended into Heaven. This tells something about the "how" of His return. It is important that our concepts of the second coming be informed by the revelation from Scripture rather than by the opinions of men. Bookstore shelves overflow today with the latter.

The late evangelist, Charles Reign Scoville, once spoke of the danger of misinformation. At the close of one of his city-wide meetings, he was waiting for a train in Defiance, Michigan. He saw, not far from the railway station, a blacksmith shop. What caught his eye was the sign in front of the place of business. The sign advertised the smith's ability to do almost anything with metal. It read, "All kinds of twisting and turning done here." Scoville quipped that such a sign would be appropriate to hang over the pulpits where some sensationalists preach on the theme of Christ's return. All kinds of twisting and turning are done to Bible passages in the shaping of peculiar doctrines related to end times.

As we speak in these pages of the Bible promise of the Lord's return, we scrupulously will avoid divisive opinions. We rather will assert only the Biblical truth, which is affirmed by all the church, that Jesus will return.

One certain Scriptural fact is that the Lord will return "with the clouds; and every eye shall see him" (Revelation 1:7). At the ascension of Jesus "a cloud received him out of their sight" (Acts 1:9), and when He returns He will return with the clouds.

A sincere student once told me that Jesus had returned in 1914. I quoted Revelation 1:7: "Every eye shall see him." Then I was told that to "see him" means to perceive that He is here and that, if I but had eyes of faith, I would be aware that Christ had come.

Perhaps I need another lesson. I choose to stay with the church that has believed through nearly two thousand years that the same Jesus "shall so come in like manner" as the apostles "beheld him going into heaven" (Acts 1:11).

When Christ returns, He will not be alone. We have His word on that: "The Son of man shall come in his glory, and all the angels with him" (Matthew 25:31). A-L-L spells a lot of angels. John saw "ten thousand times ten thousand, and thousands of thousands" (Revelation 5:11)—and we don't know whether those were all the angels or not.

What an exciting day it will be when Jesus comes back! At "a great sound of a trumpet" the sky will be filled with angels going to "gather together his elect from the four winds, from one end of heaven to the other" (Matthew 24:31).

The Pasadena Rose Parade cannot hold a candle to the scene of Christ returning with the angels. Not only will the sky be filled with hosts of angels, but there will be a glorious radiance everywhere. Listen to Jesus: "For whosoever shall be ashamed of me and of my words, of him shall the Son of man be ashamed, when he cometh in his own glory, and the glory of the Father, and of the holy angels" (Luke 9:26). Hear that again: His own glory, the Father's glory, and the glory of the holy angels! "O that will be glory for me."

Back and forth across the sky the angels will be marching. Echoing from one end of heaven to the other will be the trumpet call. It will not be a silent or secret coming. "The Lord himself shall descend from heaven, with a shout, with the voice of the archangel, and with the trump of God" (1 Thessalonians 4:16).

How will Christ return? He will return with the clouds, with the angels, with glory, and with a shout and trumpet call. We have compared that coming with a colorful parade, but the parallel is imperfect. You can line the streets of your city for a parade. You know when it is scheduled to pass by. But the time of Christ's coming is not announced in advance. "Of that day and hour knoweth no one" (Matthew 24:36).

The Purpose of His Coming

We are content with the Bible answer to the question of how or in what manner Jesus will return. Can we be satisfied with the Scriptural answer to the question of why or for what reason He will be coming back? The purpose of His coming can be seen in the events that will accompany it. He will come to bring these things to pass. What are they? We turn to the Bible and the Bible alone for our answer:

> But we would not have you ignorant, brethren, concerning them that fall asleep; that ye sorrow not, even as the rest, who have no hope. For if we believe that Jesus died and rose again, even so them also that are fallen asleep in Jesus will God bring with him. For this we say unto you by the word of the Lord, that we that are alive, that are left unto the coming of the Lord, shall in no wise precede them that are fallen asleep. For the Lord himself shall descend from heaven, with a shout, with the voice of the archangel, and with the trump of God: and the dead in Christ shall rise first; then we that are alive, that are left, shall together with them be caught up in the clouds, to meet the Lord in the air: and so shall we ever be with the Lord. Wherefore comfort one another with these words.
> —1 Thessalonians 4:13-18

Paul made it clear to the Thessalonians that a major event associated with Christ's return would be the resurrection of the dead. He did the same for the Corinthians in his first letter to them.

> We shall all be changed, in a moment, in the twinkling of an eye, at the last trump: for the trumpet shall sound, and the dead shall be raised incorruptible.
>
> —1 Corinthians 15:51, 52

What kind of a resurrection body can we expect who "wait for a Saviour, the Lord Jesus Christ"? (Philippians 3:20). The reply is that He "shall fashion anew the body of our humiliation, that it may be conformed to the body of his glory" (Philippians 3:21).

I am not ashamed to admit my inability to explain in full what a Christian's resurrection body will be like. Not even Christ's intimate apostles could give a full answer. John wrote,

> Behold what manner of love the Father hath bestowed upon us, that we should be called children of God; and such we are. . . . Beloved, now are we children of God, and it is not yet made manifest what we shall be. We know that, if he shall be manifested, we shall be like him; for we shall see him even as he is.
>
> —1 John 3:1, 2

When Jesus comes again the Christian's grave will open and the body will be raised and changed for the new world. Do the Scriptures that give such hope to believers have any word regarding the lost? Will they ever rise? Here is Jesus' answer:

> The hour cometh, in which all that are in the tombs shall hear his voice, and shall come forth; they that have done good, unto the resurrection of life; and they that have done evil, unto the resurrection of judgment.
>
> —John 5:28, 29

The general resurrection prepares for the Judgment Day. Try to visualize the scene. God is on the throne, and all men who have ever lived are brought before Him. The book of Revelation pulls back the curtain to reveal that encounter between the Maker and His creation: "I saw the dead, the great and the small, standing before the throne; and books were opened" (Revelation 20:12).

"Books" are opened, not just one book. Do you suppose one book may be the record of your life, written by some recording angel? Perhaps another book may be the teaching of Jesus, which will be the standard for man's "final exam." Church treasurers may suggest that bank books may reveal a great deal about where a person has placed his real interest.

One thing more certain is that "every knee" shall bow (Philippians 2:10). In accepting the Savior the redeemed have voluntarily bowed in acknowledgment of Jesus' lordship over their lives. But on this occasion, after the day of salvation has passed and the Day of Judgment has begun, the knees of atheists and infidels, libertines and skeptics, shall bow in admission that they have been wrong.

Finally, "if any was not found written in the book of life, he was cast into the lake of fire" (Revelation 20:15). The words of Christ will be, "Depart from me, ye cursed, into the eternal fire which is prepared for the devil and his angels" (Matthew 25:41). How much we would rather hear the words to the saved: "Come, ye blessed of my Father, inherit the kingdom prepared for you from the foundation of the world" (Matthew 25:34).

Why will Christ return? Other answers may be gleaned from the pages of Scripture, but these will suffice. The events tied to His coming will be the resurrection, the final judgment, and the consummation of world history with its ushering in of eternity. Immediately after John tells of the judgment scene, he seeks to describe the "new heaven and new earth" with the "new Jerusalem" (Revelation 21:1—22:5).

Hear Peter's confirming teaching: "The day of the Lord will come as a thief; in the which the heavens shall pass away with a great noise, and the elements shall be dissolved with fervent heat, and the earth and the works that are therein shall be burned up. . . . But, according to his promise, we look for new heavens and a new earth, wherein dwelleth righteousness" (2 Peter 3:10, 13).

After Christ comes no time remains for earthly kingdoms. No place abides on this old planet for rebuilt temples. "When the trumpet of the Lord shall sound," then "time shall be no more," and the morning shall break "eternal, bright, and fair."

The Time of His Coming

As to when Christ is coming, we are aware that no one on earth has that information. Some may think they do, and have the charts to prove it. But many date-setters have learned the hard way that "of that day and hour knoweth no one, not even the angels of heaven" (Matthew 24:36).

The people of earth will not be able to predict the day by some obvious sign of forewarning. Jesus compared the final day to the coming of the flood in the time of Noah. That generation had Noah's word that a flood was coming, but nothing in nature kept them from regular meals or from sending out wedding announcements and planning new families (Matthew 24:37-42).

Jesus said again and again that the time of His coming is not revealed to us: "Ye know not on what day your Lord cometh" (Matthew 24:42). "Be ye also ready; for in an hour that ye think not the Son of man cometh" (Matthew 24:44). "Ye know not the day nor the hour" (Matthew 25:13). Yet, while men and angels have not been informed as to the day of Christ's return, the day has been set. God "hath appointed a day in which he will judge the world" (Acts 17:31).

In 1712 a man predicted the appearance of a new comet in the sky on October 12. He also foretold the return of Jesus within the week. Many people knew their Bibles too well to take the date-setter seriously. They knew that "not even the angels of heaven" were that fully informed. They laughed at the prediction. However, when October 12, 1712, revealed the new comet in the heavens, their minds changed to believe that a prophet correct in one prediction might be right in the other. Some folk paid off long-standing bills so that failure to pay would not be held against them. Some who were living together out of wedlock became very nervous about their situation.

Jesus did not come in 1712, but He may come today. Are we living by the will of God? The time to be concerned is now. It is not after fear drives us to do what is not really our desire.

I have a clipping in my file from the Portland, Oregon, *Journal*. It tells of Orson Welles' long-ago radio broadcast about men from Mars attacking the country. The fictitious production was so realistic that at least two people in Grants Pass, Oregon, rushed to the preacher's house requesting baptism. That became a front-page story. If we are not secure in our relationship with God, we should be thinking about it now, not at some frightening day in the future.

The Preparation for His Coming

In whatsoever way Christ comes back, we will be in on all His blessings if we are redeemed. Whysoever He returns, the saved will be raised, vindicated at the judgment, and brought into the holy city of the new world. Whensoever Jesus' second advent occurs, the time matters not to those who are ready.

All of this is true, and that means that the question of prime importance is what is to be done to become ready.

Brevity and clarity are fitting qualities to the answer of such a vital question. The Christian is to live a Christian life and render Christian service.

"Everyone that hath this hope set on him purifieth himself, even as he is pure," writes John (1 John 3:3). "Seeing that these things are thus all to be dissolved, what manner of persons ought ye to be in all holy living and godliness," admonished Peter (2 Peter 3:11). "Trade . . . till I come," said Jesus in a parable (Luke 19:13). "Let us hope and trust, let us watch and pray, and labor till the Master comes," sings the hymn-writer.

The non-Christian becomes ready by coming to Christ so that the record of sins against him may be removed.

In the year 1880 there was a horrible theater fire in New York City. A man walked onto the stage to inform the people: "Ladies and gentlemen, the theater is on fire. Remain calm, but walk quietly and in good order to the exits and no one will be hurt."

The people began to do as instructed, taking their coats and hats with them. At this point another person mounted the platform, cupped his hands and shouted to the crowd, "Ladies and gentlemen, take your seats. That was just a part of the play."

Back into their seats the audience slipped in embarrassment. But then, onto the stage from dressing rooms below, rushed actors and actresses with garments afire. As one uncontrolled mob, the viewers raced for the exits and trampled many.

Lives were lost unnecessarily because a foolish person shouted, "Don't get excited, ladies and gentlemen. It is just a part of the play."

When people think of getting right with God, are some of them kept from making their decision because mothers and fathers, neighbors or friends, tell them that the preacher's warnings are "just a part of the play"?

The fact is that Jesus will come again (John 14:3). The truth is that "we must all be made manifest before the judgment-seat of Christ; that each one may receive the things done in the body" (2 Corinthians 5:10). The plea is "Be ye also ready; for in an hour that ye think not the Son of man cometh" (Matthew 24:44).

A Hawaiian musician by the name of Sol Hopi was converted to Christ many years ago in Los Angeles. His conversion meant also the conversion of his voice and the transformation of his guitar into an instrument for the Lord to use. One gospel song he penned and sang was about the promise of Christ's return.

> When Jesus comes this earth will shake
> and hearts will quake.
> Be ready.
>
> When Jesus comes His face we'll see
> eternally.
> Be ready.
>
> Has your soul been filled with God's love
> and Holy Ghost?
> Are you saved and ready to meet
> the Lord of hosts?
>
> When Jesus comes, don't hesitate,
> don't be too late.
> Be ready.

That is good advice. I'm going to follow it. I hope you will follow it too.

13

Victory over

the first enemy
Doubt

the present enemy
Detour

the last enemy
Death

13

The Promise of Victory

Count the number of times the word *victory* appears in this excerpt from chapter 15 of First Corinthians:

> Then shall come to pass the saying that is written, Death is swallowed up in victory. O death, where is thy victory? O death, where is thy sting? The sting of death is sin; and the power of sin is the law: but thanks be to God, who giveth us the victory through our Lord Jesus Christ.
> —1 Corinthians 15:54-57

Did you hear three times in those few sentences the word *victory*? It was "victory . . . victory . . . victory!"

I am reminded of an incident that took place in Oregon about forty years ago. Tape recorders had not been invented yet. Lester Marsh was an elder in the church I served. He played for me some records he recently had cut on his equipment. It was a new machine that he had received for his birthday. Wanting to experiment with his new tool, he had turned on his radio to inscribe on the wax disc both music and speeches.

What 1 Corinthians 15:54-57 brings to memory is the record that Mr. Marsh had made of a speech by Winston Churchill addressing the House of Commons. The record had been broken. When the speech was drawing to a close, and you visualized Great Britain's leader making the V for victory sign with his fingers, the broken record began to say, "And we shall have victory, victory, victory, victory, victory." On and on it went.

The broken record sounded much like God's inspired record that shall never be broken. The Bible promise is victory, victory, victory. Victory over sin! Victory over the grave! Victory over death! Victory over hell! Victory through our Lord Jesus Christ!

"In all these things we are more than conquerors through him that loved us" (Romans 8:37). That means victory for you.

"But thanks be unto God, who always leadeth us in triumph in Christ" (2 Corinthians 2:14). That means victory for you.

"And they overcame him [Satan] because of the blood of the Lamb" (Revelation 12:11). That means victory for you.

"Be of good cheer; I have overcome the world" (John 16:33). That means victory for you. Victory over all enemies from the first enemy to the last enemy. That is the victory promised.

Death: The Last Enemy

Paul declared in 1 Corinthians 15 that the risen and ascended Christ "must reign, till he hath put all his enemies under his feet." He then named the specific, final enemy: "The last enemy that shall be abolished is death" (1 Corinthians 15:25, 26).

Note the wonder of this promise. The entire fifteenth chapter of the letter to Corinth is given to this subject. In verses 1-11 the resurrection is asserted to be a part of "the gospel." Christ's resurrection "on the third day" was not a thing unheard of, but "according to the scriptures" of old. No historical fact was better established than Jesus' rising from the grave. Many witnesses saw Him alive after His death.

Verses 12-19 explain how vain would be the church's hope without this central doctrine that Christ arose. Verses 20-28 center on the promise that "as in Adam all die, so also in Christ shall all be made alive." Verses 29-34 assert that since Christians face death daily, it would be foolish to follow Christ into death if we were not certain that we would follow Him in resurrection. The last half of the chapter describes the nature of the resurrection body and fills the reader with the certainty of this hope.

What a comfort this chapter has been through the Christian centuries! What sad occasions have been turned into times of rejoicing!

What hymnody and poetry have been inspired by the thought of this promise that "in a moment, in the twinkling of an eye, at the last trump . . . the dead shall be raised incorruptible, and we shall be changed" (1 Corinthians 15:52).

With God's Word giving assurance, we can turn to the casket that is being lowered into the grave and find our hearts repeating Fitz-Green Halleck's poetic words of conviction:

> "Goodbye till morning come again."
> We part, if part we must, with pain,
>   But night is short and hope is sweet;
>   Faith fills our heart and wings our feet,
> And so we sing the old refrain,
> "Goodbye till morning come again."

As we note the wonder of this divine promise, it is important to note the words Paul uses. He is writing as a Christian to Christian Corinthians. In their background is the Platonic thought that permeated all of Achaia.

Greeks acquainted with philosophy would not be used to thinking of death as an enemy, as Paul labels it in 1 Corinthians 15:26. More likely they heard death spoken of as a friend. Plato considered the body as the prison house of the soul. In most Greek thinking material things were evil. That meant even human bodies were considered to be evil. Suicide was one option considered open to any man wanting to be freed from his terrible body.

The Christian teaching of creation, incarnation, and resurrection contradicted such thinking. If God created the material world, can it be as evil as the philosophers thought? If Jesus took on flesh and dwelt among us, did He not show that man was worth redeeming? If God promises a resurrection body, then He will raise the body and transform it. The death of the body is an enemy, but it is an enemy that will be overcome.

That means we shall live forever. With that assurance we can bypass some of the questions that trouble scholars. When shall we see the mysterious millennium described in Revelation 20:1-6? Who will live in the new earth we read about in 2 Peter 3:13 and Revelation 21:1? Why will the sea be no more? (Revelation 21:1). In this short chapter we cannot even mention all the different answers that have been given to these and other questions. Sometime we shall know fully, but not now (1 Corinthians 13:12).

Just now let us think rather of what is made plain. We shall live in new Jerusalem. God will be there. Pain and sorrow will be gone along with death. We shall serve God, and we shall see His face (Revelation 21:1-4; 22:3-5). What more could we ask for all eternity?

Doubt: The First Enemy

If death is called the last enemy, there is the implication that there are other enemies to be overcome. Since death is the last enemy, what might be named the first enemy? I nominate doubt as enemy number one. Only those who have faith will know the resurrection unto life. That makes doubt an enemy and faith a friend.

Only two times in the Gospel records is Jesus said to have marvelled. Once it was because of doubt residing in Israel. The other time it was because of faith living outside Israel. At Nazareth "he marvelled because of their unbelief" (Mark 6:6). At Capernaum He met a Roman centurion. The record says that Jesus "marvelled at him, and turned and said unto the multitude that followed him, I say unto you, I have not found so great faith, no, not in Israel" (Luke 7:9).

Faith in Christ is a marvelous friend. Belief in Jesus is never an enemy. Faith has always been a friend. The Old Testament saints "through faith subdued kingdoms, wrought righteousness, obtained promises" (Hebrews 11:33). Faith is to you a "shield . . . wherewith ye shall be able to quench all the fiery darts of the evil one" (Ephesians 6:16). Faith is the name of your outstretched hand that receives the salvation God graciously offers, "for by grace have ye been saved through faith" (Ephesians 2:8). Faith is the reason Christians are overcomers rather than people overcome. As it is written, "this is the victory that hath overcome the world, even our faith. And who is he that overcometh the world, but he that believeth that Jesus is the Son of God?" (1 John 5:4, 5).

Many of God's promises have faith as the stipulation. Consider the promises of prayer that are printed below. You may think of others to add to the list:

> Without faith it is impossible to be well-pleasing unto him; for he that cometh to God must believe that he is, and that he is a rewarder of them that seek after him.
> —Hebrews 11:6

> If any of you lacketh wisdom, let him ask of God, who giveth to all liberally and upbraideth not; and it shall be given him. But let him ask in faith, nothing doubting: for he that doubteth is like the surge of the sea driven by the wind and tossed. For let not that man think that he shall receive anything of the Lord; a doubleminded man, unstable in all his ways.
> —James 1:5-8

When the apostles failed in casting out a demon from an epileptic boy, they privately asked Jesus, "Why could not we cast it out?" Jesus said, "Because of your little faith" (Matthew 17:19-20). After withering a fig tree, Jesus dispelled Peter's questionings with this explanation: "Have faith in God. . . . I say unto you, All things whatsoever ye pray and ask for, believe that ye receive them, and ye shall have them" (Mark 11:22, 24).

Faith is a friend. Doubt is an enemy. That is true whether you consider the promise of prayer or the promise of salvation. The jailor at Philippi asked Paul and Silas what he must do to find salvation. They replied, "Believe on the Lord Jesus, and thou shalt be saved" (Acts 16:31). Those desiring baptism in the early days of the church were not indiscriminately immersed. They were told, "If thou believest with all thy heart, thou mayest." Those affirming, "I believe that Jesus Christ is the Son of God" went down into the water (Acts 8:37, 38). Those seeking salvation confessed with the mouth that Jesus was Lord, but the confession had to come from one who believed in his heart that God raised Him from the dead (Romans 10:9, 10). To Nicodemus Jesus explained, "God so loved the world, that he gave his only begotten son, that whosoever believeth on him should not perish" (John 3:16).

Paul's pride in the gospel was based on the fact that "it is the power of God unto salvation to every one that believeth." Christianity has to do with "a righteousness of God from faith unto faith: as it is written, But the righteous shall live by faith" (Romans 1:16, 17).

If belief sets you on the way to life, what results from doubt? The commission of worldwide gospel preaching assures that "he that believeth and is baptized shall be saved; but he that disbelieveth shall be condemned" (Mark 16:16). Seeing doubt as an enemy, we need to consider the disciple we call "doubting Thomas." Jesus brought such evidence to him that he could not remain in unbelief. The risen Lord appeared to him and said, "Reach hither thy finger, and see my hands; and reach hither thy hand, and put it into my side: and be not faithless, but believing." Thomas ever after was a man of unswerving conviction that Jesus was "Lord and . . . God." The benediction of Christ follows: "Because thou hast seen me, thou hast believed: blessed are they that have not seen, and yet have believed" (John 20:26-29).

Modern "doubting Thomases" need evidence to produce faith, and the credible testimony that Christ is risen comes to them in written form. As the last apostle on earth declared, "these [miracles] are written that ye may believe that Jesus is the Christ, the Son of God; and that believing ye may have life in his name" (John 20:31). God prescribed eyewitness testimony as the cure for doubt.

> Whosoever shall call upon the name of the Lord shall be saved. How then shall they call on him in whom they have not believed? and how shall they believe in him whom they have not heard? and how shall they hear without a preacher? . . . How beautiful are the feet of them that bring glad tidings of good things. . . . So belief cometh of hearing.
> —Romans 10:13-15, 17

As Jesus prayed for all who would believe on Him down to the end of Christian history, He knew what would produce their faith. He prayed, "Neither for these [apostles] only do I pray, but for them also that believe on me through their word" (John 17:20).

The links in the chain go together. Jesus began His ministry preaching, "The time is fulfilled, and the kingdom of God is at hand: repent ye, and believe in the gospel" (Mark 1:15). At the end of His ministry He still was calling for faith: "Believe in God, believe also in me" (John 14:1). Christ arose, and His deity was established. Witnesses of the fact gave their testimony to the fact. Faith in that testimony produced the church.

Detour: The Present Enemy

We have a last enemy called death, and it will be overcome by the bodily resurrection at Christ's return. We have a first enemy named doubt, and it can be overcome by the abundant evidence to Christ's deity given in the apostolic testimony. Do we have a present enemy that needs to be recognized to be conquered?

There is such an enemy. Local congregations need to be aware. Christian schools established to fulfill a particular mission need to be alerted. Individual believers need to watch for this foe. The present enemy wears the name *Detour*.

Have you ever known of a believer who got sidetracked from the faith? Have you heard of a person who overcame the enemy of doubt and confessed Christ, only to later fall away from the faith? When a seminary is established by Bible believers to raise up a ministry that has solid convictions, do you realize it may some day have professors in its classrooms denying the very essentials of the faith? People and organizations need to watch out, lest they be detoured from their purpose.

Why does the Scripture admonish us to "remember Lot's wife"? (Luke 17:32). It is because she turned back.

Why do New Testament authors call on the churches to remember what happened to God's Old Testament people, Israel? (Hebrews 3, 4). It is because they fell in the wilderness. After the deliverance from Egypt by God's outstretched hand, many people of Israel did not get to enter the promised land. Let Christians learn from this, says the author of Hebrews:

> Take heed, brethren, lest haply there shall be in any one of you an evil heart of unbelief, in falling away from the living God: but exhort one another day by day, so long as it is called To-day; lest any one of you be hardened by the deceitfulness of sin: for we are become partakers of Christ, if we hold fast the beginning of our confidence firm unto the end.
> —Hebrews 3:12-14

While you are remembering Lot's wife and Israel, also remember Demas and Hymenaeus and Judas. Demas was a co-laborer with Paul and was, to a point, a loyal friend. Yet the last page of Paul's last letter tells that Demas was derailed, diverted, detoured. It was sad to write, "Demas forsook me, having loved this present world" (2 Timothy 4:10). A few years earlier, in telling Timothy to hold fast to the faith, it was painful to add that "some having thrust [it] from them made shipwreck concerning the faith: of whom is Hymenaeus" (1 Timothy 1:19, 20). Judas not only had been a follower of Christ; he had been picked to be an apostle and had been trusted to be their treasurer. But today his fame lies in his betrayal of the one in whom he had believed.

The Bible contains too many stories of detoured lives for us to look now at them all. It tells too many, however, for us not to take the message seriously. Satan will try to turn us aside. This enemy of this present time needs to be recognized for the threat it is. The old enemy of doubt has been overcome in your present faith. The last enemy will be defeated when Christ comes for those who remain faithful. This highlights the fact that attention must presently be given to the foe of right now.

To converts the apostle to the Gentiles had left behind in Galatia, Paul found it necessary to write, "I marvel that ye are so quickly removing from him that called you" (Galatians 1:6). The positive example of Jesus' steadfastness we need to remember. Jesus never turned back from His purpose. He set His face to go to Jerusalem and die for the world (Luke 9:51). As He taught others, He lived by His own teaching: those putting their hands to the plow ought not to turn back (Luke 9:62).

The school of Christ cannot graduate dropouts. Those running the race of life must "lay aside every weight, and the sin which doth so easily beset us, and . . . run with patience the race . . . looking unto Jesus" (Hebrews 12:1, 2). No tailor will do well at his trade if he fails to tie a knot in his thread.

The book that concludes the entire sixty-six books of the Bible is the book of Revelation. A key word written there many times is the word *overcome*. Each of the seven letters to the seven churches of Asia ends with a promise to "him that overcometh." Toward the end of the book is revealed the King of kings and Lord of lords, riding forth as a warrior. He is the one who leads His army to victory in the overcoming of every enemy—including death, doubt, and detour (Revelation 19:11-16).

> Conquering now and still to conquer,
>   Rideth a King in His might!
> Leading the host of all the faithful
>   Into the midst of the fight;
> See them with courage advancing;
>   Clad in their brilliant array,
> Shouting the name of their Leader,
>   Hear them exultingly say:
> Not to the strong is the battle,
>   Not to the swift is the race,
> Yet to the true and the faithful
>   Vict'ry is promised through grace.
>   —Fanny J. Crosby

Conclusion

"For to you is the promise, and to your children, and to all that are afar off, even as many as the Lord our God shall call unto him" (Acts 2:39). What Peter said to his hearers regarding the promise of salvation, I write to you regarding the promises we have been considering in this volume. Each promise is from God. Each promise is to you. Each promise is from God, to you, with love.

"Man shall not live by bread alone" (Mathew 4:4). God's Word provides us with the bread from Heaven that satisfies the hungering soul. Feast on the promises the Lord has provided. Drink deeply at the refreshing fountain of Jesus' gospel. Christ Jesus, God's Son, is the only one who can say to you, "I am the bread of life; he that cometh to me shall not hunger, and he that believeth on me shall never thirst" (John 6:35).

"Oh taste and see that Jehovah is good" (Psalm 34:8). Each promise is a doorway of hope. Enter into life.